Zen
and the art of
Post-Modern Canada

In the same series :

A Mess That Deserves a Big NO, by Pierre Elliott Trudeau
The Last Cod-Fish, by Pol Chantraine
The Traitor and the Jew, by Esther Delisle
Seven Fateful Challenges for Canada, by Deborah Coyne

Canadian Cataloguing in Publication Data
Schecter, Stephen, 1946-
    Zen and the art of Post-Modern Canada : Does the Trans-Canada
    Highway always lead to Charlottetown?

    (Food for thought ; 3)
    Includes bibliographical references.

    ISBN 1-895854-03-2

    1. Canada - Constitutional law.   2. Canada - Politics and government -
1984-   . 3. Consensus Report on the Constitution (1992).   4. Federal-
provincial relations - Canada.   I. Title   II. Series: Food for thought (Montréal, Quebec) ; 3.

JL65.S24 1993   342.71'03   C93-096476-4

If you wish to receive our lists of forthcoming titles,
please send your request to the following address :
Robert Davies Publishing,
P.O.B. 702, Outremont, QC, Canada H2V 4N6

Stephen Schecter

Zen
and the art of
Post-Modern Canada

Does the Trans-Canada Highway
always lead to Charlottetown?

ROBERT DAVIES PUBLISHING
MONTREAL – TORONTO

DISTRIBUTED IN CANADA BY

Stewart House,
481 University Avenue, Suite 900
Toronto, Ontario M5G 2E9

☎ *(Ontario & Québec) 1-800-268-5707*
(rest of Canada) 1-800-268-5742
Fax 416-940-3642

1   2   3   4   1993   1994   1995

Table of Contents

PART

ONE

1

FOR A LONG TIME I DID NOT REALIZE *This Land Is Your Land* was a song about Canada. I guess I must have unconsciously known it was first written about the United States. Then a friend of mine told me that when Arlo Guthrie and Pete Seeger got hold of the song, they changed the words once more so they would apply to the entire planet. Which makes the song one more thing Canada borrowed before disappearing.

I liked that song. I sang the words "From Nova Scotia to Vancouver Island" with great feeling, knowing nothing of either place and not stopping to think that Nova Scotia should have been Newfoundland. Eventually they did replace it with Bonavista, but I was much older by the time I learned that version. One day I got to Golden in the B.C. Rockies and finally knew what "ribbon of highway" and "purple valleys" meant. But then life is like that, isn't it? Always finding out in retrospect what you were heading for. So, as they say in that other national language, *au lendemain du référendum*, what was it we were aiming at on the road to Charlottetown, 1992?

A crack-up, some would say. Did. A monumental crack-up. And something did crack. Not the country, since we're still here, but we did have a brush with one of the black angel's derivatives. There is a lull now, but it won't last. The unfinished business won't let it, although it may well be that the constitutional business today is unfinished by nature. Still, we ought to look at matters a bit before we are again taken, surprisingly, by surprise. Unlike love, there is no reason to suppose it will be lovelier the second time around.

Think of the country like a teacup with a fault line in it, a moral fault line. One day it might simply give way. On the other hand, we could go on a long time with nothing cataclysmic happening. Last October the crack got a little wider, but so what? Joe Clark did not immediately resign, wringing his conscience like a clothes-line. The Royal still does okay at the bank. I am alive and well and writing you from Québec, though I still hear the woman from Nova Scotia I heard on the radio the day after the referendum, explaining why she voted yes. Her small voice spoke generous words. Fearless, reasonable, she wanted to tell the people of Québec she wanted them in Confederation. Yes, she knew there were faults with the accord, but what accord did not have them? Life is complicated, is it not, and there are times when one has to weigh the good and the bad and go for the overall balance. Native peoples were getting some of their grievances redressed in a major way, Québec was being recognized as a distinct partner in Confederation; the woman from Nova Scotia could allow herself to think she would close her eyes on a legacy to her children that she had once inherited herself. But that was the grand and noble view coming from Nova Scotia, the timber province of Canada, proud and patrician and perhaps the most Canadian of them all. It produced Bob Stanfield. Eric Kierans now lives in that part of the Maritimes, whence he talks to us on the radio. A wonderful real estate agent in Montréal I know has a summer house there, and thinking of her I think of elegance and the waves lapping the shore in Cape Breton, another place I have not been to. Perhaps that's the problem with Canada. We haven't been to enough of it, so it remains a country of the imagination. This land is your land, from Nova Scotia to anywhere.

Elias Canetti, one of this century's great thinkers, wrote in his book, *Crowds and Power*, that every nation has a national crowd symbol, a deep metaphor that sums up its collective existence, defines in some striking imagery what binds its members. The sea, for example, for England.

Dykes for Holland. A marching forest for Germany. Italy, he wrote, coming to nationhood late, has no such symbol, except for ancient Rome which is full of empty ruins. In this void the Fascists tried to impose one but failed; theirs was a false crowd symbol. The case of Italy is interesting, for it is somewhat like Canada's. What would be ours? The maple leaf? But a leaf flutters and dies with every autumn. Is that why it is our best approximation, a symbol of constantly renewable federalism? Its very lightness, however, should give pause for reflection. Lester Pearson's attempt to present Canada with a symbol of national unity was greeted with typically Canadian near self-effacement: polite applause. In Québec it never took hold. The national crowd symbol here still remains *la conquête*, the presence of the *fleur de lys* even on underwear notwithstanding. In that respect the Parti Québécois has the same difficulty Lester Pearson had. We are a country without a sense of being one. To our great merit perhaps, we are a vast piece of tundra that exists for real only in our individual imaginations.

When I was younger than I was when I first learned *This Land Is Your Land*, I used to love hearing the story *Paddle-to-the-Sea*. It was the story of a wooden canoe with its wooden Indian figure seated inside it as it voyaged from the source of Lake Superior to the Atlantic Ocean, a kind of *coureur du bois* in reverse. There was much danger on the way, the most scary to my child's eye being the drop at the Sault Ste. Marie locks. One day I made it to Sault Ste. Marie, and of course the perspective had changed. But to this day, if you ask me what Canada is, I might well answer it is the trajectory of a wooden Indian canoe on its way from a vast hinterland of snow and trees to the sea beyond the river. The trajectory is like water itself, slippery, rushing, cannot be grasped, and the country feels like that, one long continuous fade on the silver screen of my consciousness. Diaphanous; the first nation itself a people of mythical stature, living up north, land of the never setting sun we stand on guard for, only its rays captured on canvas in the Tom Thomson paintings at the National Gallery. Jack Pine on Lake Superior.

It would seem, however, that is not enough. It is not enough to live in a country certain in the knowledge you have seen it without travelling across it, because that is its nature. Not enough to have seen Mr. Esso on Hockey Night in Canada, dreamed of Alberta north of Edmonton as the Imperial sign ovals out on the tube. Not enough to have read Margaret Laurence in order to smell Qu'Appelle. Not even enough to laugh with Irving Layton about love where the nights are long, always waiting for that love, that night, no sisters of mercy, and a '68 Buick revving up its engine in a Réjean Ducharme novel. Post auto-pact Canada. Hyper-real. South of Wawa.

So we decided to give ourselves a constitution. The legal experts will tell you we already have one, but Prime Minister Mulroney was not interested in the technical aspects when he decided he'd bring Québec into the Canadian family. Former Prime Minister Trudeau would tell you Québec was never out of it, which was Mr. Mulroney's first mistake. But there is a sense in which Mr. Mulroney was right. He wanted Canadians to make a commitment to some articulated version of themselves, decide that their composite parts constituted a country they could symbolically represent to themselves. Unfortunately, he never came across with that message, never gave it substance in other than procedural terms. Québec hadn't signed the 1982 document, it was important that it sign one a decade later. If Canada was many parts, it was also the sum of its parts. A shopping list as a national crowd symbol?

Only the times were not right. Too much cross-border shopping. Too many groups wanting to join the fray and write their demands into the constitution. Over it all presiding a well-intentioned labour lawyer understandably mistaking the noble art of politics for an exercise in collective bargaining. So we got a post-modern document, concocted in post-modern style and rejected in post-modern fashion. This book is its story: why, what, how post-modern? That we may understand a bit about our times and our country. There is at least that to be gained from last year's paroxysm.

2

WILFRED LAURIER ONCE SAID the twentieth century belonged to Canada. It hasn't quite turned out that way, but the Charlottetown accord was a first of its kind, for it was the first time an advanced industrial nation tried to give itself a constitution. Some people might dispute the advanced industrial nation title, but in spite of a declining manufacturing sector, free trade, and other features of a post-industrial syndrome, Canada still attends the G7 meetings. Its standard of living, all things considered, is one of the highest in the world. People from all over would not mind living here. They'd even be willing to brave our winters, which says something about our attractiveness, and not only because they think they will eventually get to spend them in Florida or Hawaii. If Michael Ondaatje is anything to go by, I'd say the country would do well with thirty million new immigrants, but that's another story we'll come to in time.

That wise political thinker, Hannah Arendt, pointed out in her study *On Revolution*, that constitutions refer to the act of foundation. In drawing up a constitution one is setting out the basic law of the land, the fundamental rules that govern a society and at the same time codify what it is, what constitutes it as a sovereign political body. A constitution in that sense is unlike any other set of laws a society may legislate, for it sets the framework within which laws shall be enacted and, if disliked, challenged; ultimately, even declared unconstitutional. In her discussion of the French Revolution, she pointed out that the great actors of 1789 were never able to give the revolution a permanent functioning set of institutions. In spite of all their heroic efforts at constitution building, they could never lay the foundations for the new order after having thrown over the old. Hence the dynamic of continuous revolution which characterized the aftermath of the Tennis Court Oath, until finally Napoléon put a stop to it with his *coup d'état* of 1799. The first republic ended up an empire. Such was the fate of the last and most momentous political revolution of modernity. Being the last, it was also the most self-conscious, which is why we often refer to it as the emblem of modern revolution. Its relatively late appearance on the stage of history, however, one hundred and fifty years after the English Revolution and even more after the Dutch, made it also a presage of things to come. What was to come, as the very words imply, was post-modern.

It might surprise some people to read that the French Revolution was the last of the modern revolutions. What about the Russian Revolution? they might ask. What about the Chinese? And the revolutions that failed? They belong to another era, is what, however much they cloak themselves in the garb of the one that spun Edmund Burke's reflections and a tale of two cities. The French Revolution was eminently political, sought to elaborate its own foundations in the name of secular principles transcending the entire society, the state included. Nothing and no one were to be above the law, but the citizen had responsibilities to the nation that rested on the common exercise of law and reason in the pursuit of a well-ordered community. This was the condensed epitome of modern, or bourgeois, society whose origins preceded the French Revolution by three centuries. Think of the Renaissance, Hobbes and Locke, Hume and Kant, modern science we call classical when discussing Newton's physics, Descartes, Molière, Shakespeare. As a certain part of European society threw off the shackles of tradition, a new form of living came into being; rationalist, secular, urban, literate, and often Protestant. Indeed, Luther's Reformation would have been unthinkable without the printing press and a bourgeoisie to read it. And the modern state, as a political community of citizens independent of their religious beliefs, unthinkable without the Reformation.

By the time Oliver Cromwell became the reluctant leader of a revolution of saints, a whole new way of thinking about the world had opened up. The earth revolved around the sun and the government around the rights of its subjects, if only the right to worship differently, and if only as expressed in Parliament. It took nearly another half-century for the right of nonconformity to get established in English life. When it did, it happened through their version of a quiet revolution referred to in the history books as glorious. Quiet as this event might have been, it was highly significant, for one of the hallmarks of modernity was its political capacity for inclusion. Whereas previously society was much more homogeneous, integrated by authority structures that allowed for a hierarchy of reciprocal obligations within a common religion — serf to noble, one estate to the next — bourgeois society was integrated primarily through its political structure, a constitutional state that limited the arbitrary power of the sovereign because such power was incompatible with the free assembly of citizens to make laws and direct the affairs of the nation. And human beings were free because they were basically beings endowed with reason. Reason flowed through the world like a natural law, anchoring action and thought in a secular unity that made it possible to turn revolution into a new social order.

One of the characteristics of this new social order in which political institutions replaced religion as the principal sovereign agent was that henceforth citizens of different religious persuasions could inhabit the same country. The Thirty Years' War was the last time European powers went to war over issues of religion. In separating Church and State, bourgeois society was carrying out the first of many separations and thereby signalling its novelty as a political mode of social organization. This meant that it was within the political order, and notably the state, that different sectors of social activity emerged as distinct institutional spheres with their own roles and rules of behaviour. The market, science, the family, art, all emerged as separately organized spheres of activity that developed their own logic. Economic activity was no longer limited to domestic production and residence. The market dissolved the old ties of person and land, making property private and alienable and workers free to seek employment where they could find it. Private property, contract and the juridical rights of the person emerged simultaneously yet separately, bringing with it a new society and a new set of problems, or contradictions. Similarly, modern science emerged as a discipline rooted in mathematics and experimentation, while modern art developed a whole new world of representation with its own aesthetic canons. In the end, its more extreme versions hurled art like an insult in the face of the bourgeois society that had spawned it.

The possibilities for the emergence of these spheres of activity as separate institutional orders within society lay with its fundamentally political character. The modern state, founded on reason, created through law and revolution the basis for what my colleague Michel Freitag has called the capacity for institutionalization which distinguishes modernity from earlier epochs. Henceforth, each sphere could develop within a framework of relative autonomy. The family was not the state, the public was not the private. A market had its own operating rules, ways of dividing up labour, honouring contracts, running businesses, that were different from the rules governing political behaviour, family life, art and science. And yet, there was an overarching unity. All roads led to the political-legal order that sanctioned these developments in the name of reason, progress, even happiness, as Jeremy Bentham was to try to explain in his theory of utilitarianism. There was, to put it in more familiar terms, a social contract.

Often presumed, often looked for by the philosophers of the Enlightenment, this social contract implied that despite the positing of individual freedoms and the potential conflicts between these separate spheres of social activity, the society held together. What held it together was the acknowledgment, reinforced by practice, that there were outer limits to these new arrangements. They had been encouraged in order to create a new world of freedom and progress bounded by reason. These outer limits, the boundary values of the society, held as long as the political arena exercised ultimate jurisdiction in the determination of what went. As long as the people's chosen representatives could decide in Parliament the scope of what the different institutional orders could and could not do, and decide by invoking, consciously or tacitly, the agreed upon conventions of bourgeois society. There are natural limits to human endeavour. Reason knows them. So even bourgeois society recognized that to every thing there is a season and a time to every purpose under heaven.

To some, however, this state of affairs was rather fragile, carried within it the seeds of its own destruction. Marx, among others, offered the most trenchant version of the inevitable collapse of bourgeois society, but Marx was not alone. Other thinkers, in different ways, came to similar conclusions. Essentially, their argument rested on the recognition that modernity had opened a Pandora's box. Once society had been reorganized on the basis of human freedom, the exercise of autonomous capacity in the world, there was no limit to what could ensue. Once different spheres of social activity had hollowed out their own areas of jurisdiction and behaviour, what was to stop them from escaping all social restraint? Eventually, each bit of civil society, like each subordinate group, would demand its rights to develop as it saw fit, arguing that democracy and pluralism placed no fetters on the human capacity to innovate and assert new forms of self-realization. In the end, progress for every part of society implied progress for the whole, reversing what had been the case at the outset of modernity. Instead of the political centre determining socially accepted and valid behaviour, the multiple groups and sectors throughout the social order, each claiming their place in the sun and their right to proceed as they see fit, impose their agenda on the political arena. The tail now wags the dog.

To try and put it another way: let us say that in premodern times the idea of God served as the bedrock of social life. The seasons turned within a fixed order, and people lived and died without moving, for the most part, more than a few kilometres from home in a lifetime. There was a static quality to traditional life that changed with the advent of modernity. As Max Weber explained when describing the first modern entrepreneurs, a new way of doing business emerged with rational capitalism: methodical, systematic, very much in line with ascetic Calvinism. Indeed, Weber argued that the original pursuit of acquisitive gain in the sixteenth and seventeenth centuries received its consecration from the Puritan variant of Protestantism. He wondered, however, what would happen when accumulation was no longer pursued in order to confirm an inner sense of predestined salvation and God's handiwork in the world. He feared the rise of a soulless society in which people acted because that's how social life was organized. A market exists and requires certain forms of behaviour to which everyone must conform or perish. The value of such a society is defined in its own terms. Whatever goes is okay as long as it helps the reproduction of the system, since the ongoing functioning of society is seen as rational, productive, generating material benefits on a scale hitherto unknown. In a world in which God would ultimately be declared dead, as Nietzsche proclaimed a hundred years ago, there would be nothing left to give shape and form to human endeavour other than the will to power, the ferreting out of experience in every nook and cranny of life, until life itself became measured as the maximization of output in every sphere. Not a stone left unturned, not a thread dangling; ego plugged into every network.

Such a vision of the future, now become a reality, was read by extrapolating the dynamic that modernity unleashed. Within the confines of a political society that allowed for capital accumulation, representative government, modern art and science, the new spheres of autonomous behaviour slowly outstripped the wider moral and institutional order. This was especially so in the economic sphere, as the pioneering efforts of merchant and manufacturing capitalists gave way to the rise of the industrial age in the nineteenth century. A second revolution was born within bourgeois society, only this time it was not political but technical; hence the name industrial revolution. With it the tendencies that had slowly gained strength since the Renaissance matured, beginning the transformation of modernity into a new form of civilization which today we can call post-modern.

Although only today can we begin to see the full-fledged nature of post-modernity, its origins lie in the second half of the nineteenth century. Think of Tennyson's hero in *Locksley Hall*:

> For I dipt into the future, far as human eye could see,
> Saw the Vision of the world, and all the wonder that would be.

One can almost hear the century flexing its muscles, *la belle époque*, the Victorian age of international exhibitions and European imperialism, underpinned by an ongoing technical revolution that drilled its way into every corner of the earth and every inch of the soul. That was capitalism, not the bounded commonwealth of reason that we associate with bourgeois society and handed down to us in the classical images of Delacroix and Manet, already fuzzing over the sharp prudence and inner luxury of the Dutch masters. Capitalism meant the machine age, the market outstripping its national barriers and hunting all over the globe. Capitalism meant increasing division of labour, scientific management, time-motion studies, the transformation of human beings into the machines they worked and the commodities they produced. That was what Marx described and Charlie Chaplin caught on film; only he should have called it Post-Modern Times.

Why? Because modern capitalism, though it could not have emerged without the legal transformations that made a market in commodities and labour possible, also meant a betrayal of the bourgeois order that presided over its birth. Because industrial society meant the death of a bounded political order in which the central institution of society, the liberal state, held everything and everyone together. The incredible industrial expansion that marked the last half of the nineteenth century and extended into our own also shattered the moral and aesthetic sentiments, traditions and behaviour that guided modernity since 1500. The well-ordered progress that Saint-Simon, fifty years before Tennyson, dreamed would be the logical fruits of modern science, turned into the carnage of World War One. 1914 became a fateful landmark of the moral and political collapse of the bourgeoisie and the society it embodied. Yet the writing on the wall was still not clear.

Before 1914 there were already signs that some profound change was occurring in the psyche of western civilization; and what the psyche registers is what the flesh undergoes. Ideas, even if they are ahead of practice, take hold because, like Tennyson's hero, they have seen what is coming to pass. It was at the turn of the century that artists in every genre burst asunder the remaining barriers of bourgeois consciousness. Ibsen had Nora slam a door that would reverberate three quarters of a century later in every household in North America. Picasso in 1907 rocked the world with *Les demoiselles d'Avignon*, and as the art critic John Berger wrote in his essay on the moment of Cubism, seeing that picture made you feel as if the Cubists had devoured the world whole and spit it out on canvas as the devil. That was a metaphor, of course, for what Berger considered the artist's awareness that never before had the unity of the world seemed possible in non-alienated forms. In the very words of Tennyson:

> Far along the world-wide whisper of the south wind rushing warm,
> With the standards of the peoples plunging thro' the thunder-storm;
> Till the war-drum throbb'd no longer, and the battle flags were furl'd
> In the Parliament of man, the Federation of the world.

Yet precisely because of that, the failure of bourgeois society to deliver on a promise which for once seemed to be realistic produced disappointment on a monumental scale, a torn consciousness which Picasso proceeded to paint in the distorted and confused angles of a woman's body. That way of seeing the world has remained with us since: the ever-present promise of wholeness, the ever-present reality of jagged differences that will have to do for pleasure.

And so the world embraced modernism, confusing it with modernity when in fact it signalled modernity's crisis. We still like to think of ourselves as modern, especially now that everybody can go shopping at IKEA for Danish-style furniture. We are still enraptured with the cabaret that was Weimar, and indeed, that happy excitement with things radically new, experimental, hip, lit up the glowing sky of Berlin in the twenties, hiding the more sinister forces that were gathering so ostensibly in the streets. No one paid attention to Hitler when he warned that the Nazis were not to be confused with bourgeois parties. Even today too many people think nazism was a purely reactionary phenomenon, when it also marked a radically new departure in the history of the human race. Never before had a ruling group set about to exterminate, in systematic, methodical, organized fashion, another group of people defined, by its very essence, as worthy only of rational murder. The Jews were sent to their death by people who prided themselves on the efficiency with which they ran their railroads. Their sentence was approved by doctors who had already disculpated themselves in their own minds by kowtowing to forces "beyond their control". But as Freitag has also pointed out, the techniques, the logic, the organizational practices were already characteristic of an age to come. Ours.

Of course the world recovered, and for the second time in half a century launched itself on a program of reconstruction. Many think it has been a success. The brown shirts are conspicuously absent. But others are not so sure, think the world has not really confronted, and so not really overcome, the historical gash that the Nazis opened in the body politic. We have learned to refine our dynamism, made it socially acceptable, turned it to less murderous adventures. After the successive crises in the modern project the world has finally settled down to a rational program of endless expansion: material, moral, aesthetic. Every day brings new challenges, new possibilities, new decisions, and a trickle-down society brings these new horizons to the doorsteps of more and more people. It would seem that modernity has won out in the end. But consider this: what has won out is a new form of social organization, pragmatic and technical in nature, that has lost the collective moral capacity to orient its development in terms other than its own reproduction. The reconstruction is a success because it works and what works, goes. Of course, there are some problems, not least of which is the increasing level of moral and physical violence that threatens to tear the society apart. But for the moment the managers still seem to have matters under control, and this despite the fact that the managers seem less and less capable of assuming responsibility for whatever it is they manage. In short, society has become a system. Organization replaces politics. Decision-making in the managerial sense replaces the hard crunch of moral reflection and debate. And since, as Yeats put it long ago, "the centre cannot hold", everyone has a right to his or her own opinion, a code phrase for anything goes. For a world too tired or too bewildered to imagine how anyone could dare impose his or her values. It hardly seems possible that there were times when society exercised authority binding on its members.

Yet modernity was such an epoch. The society produced a version of what it was aiming at and legislated the rules which would enable it to achieve its stated goals. Its moral ends. A finality to existence which people could understand, oppose, criticize. A finality which was larger than the functional practices of the society and its constituent sectors, groups, individuals. Indeed, when modernity produced its own critics — artists, bohemians, revolutionaries — it did so because it was a society that allowed for contradictions, for discourses that contradicted, since the society was still enveloped within a wider moral universe. The various workers' movements that challenged bourgeois society did so in the name of that society's ideals. They wanted liberty and equality for everyone. Even Marx was, in that sense, a bourgeois thinker. Even today, when people grumble about the system, they often mean to criticize in this old-fashioned sense. But the choice of words is not innocent. When we grumble about the system, at some level of consciousness we must know that it is not a society with flesh and blood agents we are indicting, but an impersonal gridlock in which human agency seems to have flown out the window. Such a picture was already present in the mind of this century's foremost revolutionary, V. I. Lenin. It was he, after all, who told the socialist movement as early as 1902 that the political question was basically one of organization. It was he who said, after taking power in Russia in 1917, that socialism meant nationalization plus electrification. By that definition, every province in Canada is a socialist paradise. Without denigrating the value of our hydro companies, I should think the example would suffice to indicate why the Russian Revolution, having emerged in the shadow of industrial capitalism, is more post-modern than modern, for

it defined itself essentially in organizational terms: planning, efficiency, labour productivity. That it finally
drowned in a sea of vodka should not mislead us about its
nature. That is why the Berlin wall falling down is of less
historical import than we might at first think. Perhaps its
real lesson is, that of all the forms of post-modern organization, ours is the most efficient and hence the most
durable. It is here where the form has worked itself out at
the highest level; and so, to borrow that old phrase, since
here is the rose, here we must dance.

Which brings us back, believe it or not, to our point of
departure. The French Revolution was the last modern
revolution because it was the last that posed itself in political terms. Since then, social change has come to be seen as
a problem of social organization, social engineering, intelligent management, with democracy brought out as a bou-
quet of flowers to compliment ourselves on the real
performance. Even democracy, as we shall see next, has
lost its political kernel, hollowed out in practice to a form
of social interaction that is far from its classical origins;
and by classical one can include the eighteenth century.
This is why the failure of the French Revolution to come to
some institutionalized constitutional agreement is significant for our own dilemma. It points out the difficulty
inherent in any act of foundation, and even more when
that act occurs in times which no longer cohere in political
terms. To put it bluntly: in 1992, Canada tried to give itself
a constitutional foundation, an eminently political act,
under conditions where society no longer functions in
political terms. That was our handicap, and it proved to be
a great one. How it worked we shall see in the chapters
that follow. Before that, however, we shall need one more
digression: a brief description of what post-modern society
is, how it works, what consequences it has for people's
lives. It is one thing to say it is not a political society; it is
quite another to say it is organizational, pragmatic, technical. What does all that mean, other than to express the

idea that times have changed and they are not as they were before? Every grandparent knows that, just as he or she knows that *plus ça change, plus c'est la même chose*. So what's the big deal? Or as some people say, where's the beef?

3

THE ADVENT OF POST-MODERN society represents not only a temporal shift — what comes after modernity — but also a change in form that affects every aspect of our lives. The best way I can think of formulating this shift is to repeat that society has become a system. But what exactly is a system?

Imagine a family tree where no one ever dies. That's a kind of system; an immense bounded environment, hierarchically organized, at its top a patriarch so old he's become an abstract collection of rich information which allows the tree to keep on growing, new branches to arise unaware of their origin, concentrated now on keeping the whole shebang moving along, because not to grow is to die. Some people think of the universe as a system having neither beginning nor end, simply a system of ever-growing complexity within a mass of cold and empty space. Human beings on the planet Earth have the dubious distinction of representing the highest point of evolution in this ever-expanding system. Some people think it's absurd and write plays or treatises about the meaninglessness of life. Which is not as stupid as it seems: the philosophy of the absurd is an appropriate response to an understanding of life in systemic terms. What is the purpose of life? There doesn't seem to be any, other than to keep on truckin'.

Contemporary society is organized more and more in much the same way. Ever since the advent of the scientific management of the labour process at the turn of the century, the subdivision of social life into its component parts and their organization along the lines of rational management have proceeded apace. Hospitals, schools, governments, charities, families are all run along the principles secreted by MBA programs. Every aspect of social life has become an area of expertise. This applies not only to the big institutions that shape our lives like factories or universities, but also to the more subjective domains of existence like love and death, illness and sorrow, happiness and destiny. Think of what it means to be a parent today. A model parent, that is. One who successfully manages the multiple stages and environments of a child's development in line with the most advanced principles of psychology. One can never drive one's kids to enough movies, ballet classes, Suzuki lessons, never listen enough at the right time, counsel appropriately, intervene without intruding, protect without smothering, all in the hope that one will produce that elusive healthy normal adult, happy, fulfilled, equipped with all the inner, if not outer resources, to meet the countless challenges of tomorrow. Or think of what it means to be an accomplished individual. Once it sufficed to earn a living, have a family, build a house if you were lucky. Now one has to succeed at every one of life's stages, whose number is constantly growing. Adolescence. Pre-adolescence. Formative years. Pre-school. Pre-Sesame Street. If you don't come to kindergarten knowing how to read you have almost flunked your academic career. Soon there will be books on how to succeed as an embryo. And at the other end: mid-life crisis, post mid-life crisis, the fabulous fifties, the golden years, the declining years. How to deal with chronic illness. How to make hospital visits pleasant. How to turn death into an enriching experience. There are now degree programs at universities in thanatology, which I suppose is the science of dying. Is dying a science? An art? Do we go to school for that too?

In a society run like a system each segment is separate but integrated into the whole. It used to be that what made the segments different were their different activities, which required different norms of behaviour to fit their different purposes. Today, what makes the segments different is their sheer weight, the niche they have carved out in the social network. Kind of like CTV and CBC. Whatever they do, they all do it the same way. So institutions become organizations, integrated across the board by the procedural rules of management that the élites at the top of each organization lay down. The ways of doing things are independent of the products, services, activities specific to the organization. Universities, like factories, are measured by their outputs. The more the output the greater their success, and the greater their success the more socially useful they are deemed. It is not surprising that one president of General Motors once claimed that what was good for his company was good for America. That is exactly what managers or technocrats believe, and one can well understand how they come to believe it. If everything depends on rational management principles, then not to conform to scientific measures of organizing social life is tantamount to collective suicide. It goes against progress, utility, democracy itself; and who can be against that? Indeed, the élites atop any organization today see themselves as democratic, for it is upon their expertise that the entire edifice rests.

Yet this expertise produces strange results. For one, most of the élites disclaim any responsibility for the activities they are supposed to manage. When companies go bankrupt or governments mismanage the economy, they explain their failure in terms of forces beyond their control: the recession, international markets, global competition, as if somehow these words were supposed to explain something that did not, at the same time, call into question the usefulness of their management. That did not lead us to ask ourselves: why do we elect leaders to manage processes that cannot be managed?

Another bizarre aspect to this technocratic mania is the reference to other organizations as justification for one's own practices. Here's a little example from the university I work at. One day I get a memo on my desk from the rector. In it he explains that since the university receives over $1 million in federal contracts, it has to prove itself an equal opportunity employer. To that purpose a questionnaire will be sent round to enquire about the minority affiliations of the university's employees. Shortly thereafter the question-naire arrives on my desk. Slick, expensive, designed by the vice-rectorate for human resources, it asks us to identify our ethnic affiliation, then goes on to ask us if we belong to a visible minority, choice of eight, and an ethnic group, choice of twenty-three. The visible minority categories imply you have a skin colour various shades of brown or black and come from countries south of the latitude line that sweeps the Mediterranean. The ethnic categories are all variants of European, Jewish included. In short, an in-stitution of higher learning issues a document full of racist categories probably without even being aware of it. There are code words they have taken from other sources and they say so in the questionnaire: the Québec Human Rights Commission, Employment and Immigration Canada, Statistics Canada, as if that makes the use of these categories kosher. Since the aim of the exercise is democratic, moreover — to increase so-called minority rep-resentation in the university's employ — one could hardly accuse the same institution of being racist. They are simp-ly doing their job, applying the developed operational tech-niques to solve a social problem. The techniques were developed elsewhere and have been sanctioned by govern-ments and their watchdogs. Where's the problem?

Yet there is a problem. An institution whose task it is to produce intellectually sound categories for questionnaires such as this one winds up doing the opposite, and justifies it by invoking the *mélange* of technocratic and democratic principles that have become common usage everywhere. Indeed, they invented this procedure in the first place in order to solve a problem. Since every problem calls forth a solution, and since technocracy does not admit there are problems that cannot be solved, we wind up every day with a more complex system than the one before, and the system justifies itself. That too is a strange aspect of a society become a system. It has its own, built-in, self-evident dynamic that makes it hard to challenge. For every problem that emerges is approached operationally, pragmatically. Nothing is really solved in the end, except to create more of a mess. If, in my university, they could actually find that Filipinos were under-represented in the library, would it make a big difference? Would it be possible to rectify the situation by hiring one more, bumping off a current employee, creating a new area of conflict, possibly having a grievance lodged, avoiding that with a joint management-union committee, etc., etc.? Would not the end result have been to add a little more confusion in everyone's mind about what an ethnic group is, what rights people have, and how racist or not racist Canada, Québec, Montréal is? Perhaps the university would be able to pat itself on the back by showing it had a little bit of everyone, results of the questionnaire obliging? Whatever the outcome the society loses, just as we all lost at Charlottetown, where the situation was not all that different.

What makes this kind of operation difficult to put into question is that its logic appears in progressive language. When managers control they do not repress in the old-fashioned coercive sense. They do not appear as the exploiters of the people, fat capitalist bosses sucking our blood dry, although often enough they suck the breath out of one's soul. They present themselves, on the contrary, as the embodiment of reason, holders of specialized knowledge they would like to put at the service of the vast majority. It seems logical, since they have the entire weight of how things work on their side; and so we give them our allegiance, much as people gave theirs to priests of old, they too incumbents of social roles which conferred upon them some arcane yet indispensable competence. To the extent, moreover, that we have integrated this way of doing things into our everyday lives, that it has become part of our consciousness, our language, our way of thinking about the most intimate areas of experience, it is hard to see what is so odd about it. After all, people talk about how to manage their love lives, their careers, their domestic situations. Thus does the society become integrated at every level, from macro to micro, and so becomes a system, an integrated network of circuits that works by continuous feedback, seemingly independent of human agency. Everyone manages, no one takes responsibility. One can't even get mad at the bosses. And there's no point making a revolution, for how do you make a revolution against a system of procedures? Everyone has seen Marlon Brando in *Viva Zapata* by now.

This mode of operation, where decisions are made but no one is really responsible for them and where the guiding criterion for the decision is the feasibility of the operational procedures involved, has now struck at the very heart of the central social institution of modernity: the government. Parties move in and out of power. Governments come and go. But the procedural approach to politics triumphs across the board. It is increasingly rare for governments and parliaments to make laws and take political responsibility for the overall orientation of society such that politics becomes its normative heartland, telling its citizens that however difficult and absurd life may seem, it still has social sense, for such and such are the parameters of our common existence. Instead, the government operates like an election, one continuous free-for-all, a marketplace of competing interests in which political muscle usually forces the issue, and this despite the fact that the issue is often compromise. That merely reflects the pragmatic balance of forces within which the élites have to formulate policy. Look at the recent politics of abortion. Two competing groups of more or less equal force, each invoking rights of one kind or another. The government's response: abdicate rather than stand up and say we are for this, against that, for such and such a reason. Even when they have strong convictions they usually welsh on the delivery. Think of the moral crusader presidents south of the border. More bluster and rhetoric than anything else. Even when one side wins, one can never be sure of victory, since political decisions can be overturned when facts make it so. Hence the recourse to continuous mobilization, hence also the continuous displacement of politics from Parliament to the media. A hot line is easily worth a week in the Hansard. Your message is out there, mobilizing. Mobilizing.

There is a snag, however. A society in a state of permanent mobilization is a very precarious society. The constantly shifting consensus that results from the continuous competition of interest groups big and small, means that whatever unity exists is always created after the fact, as the end result of all those inputs. Not only is responsibility thus evaded; there is also little sense of coherence among the members of a society. One has the sense that one is engaged in permanent struggle, much like the mythical state of nature the philosophers of modernity invoked to justify constitutional government in the beginning. Only now the state of nature is not outside society but right smack in the middle, downtown and ready to ignite a social bonfire of the vanities. Some people have already started. They go into MacDonald's or universities and start shooting, often at people they don't even know.

Perhaps that's one of the downsides of technocracy. Unlike a bureaucracy, where the lines of hierarchical organization are clear, usually written and formally explicit, thus making the person at the top responsible for what his or her subordinates do, in a technocracy there is no ultimate face to the operational procedure. That's probably why parliamentarians still relish an opportunity to call for a minister's resignation — it's one of the few holdovers that still enable us to think someone will take responsibility for something. On the odd occasion when that happens, however, it is usually for reasons of personal misconduct, as if the political system were admitting no one resigns for

questions of policy, such as presiding over millions of unemployed; or a constitutional fiasco. But then, in a post-
modern society there is no more bureaucracy, not in the
classical sense. That's why it's hard to buttonhole a leader
of any organization and complain, paper in hand, "but it
says, here!", because somewhere else it also says something else, and anyway, the rules are constantly changing,
no one being able to arrest progress.

Which makes for a strange kind of progress. It used to be
that progress had a purpose. Now the purpose is progress
itself, the maintenance and reproduction of the system and
its component parts. At the individual level the story is
much the same. Progress in the quality of one's life is
defined as the maximization of one's capacity to enjoy
what is made possible, irrespective of the goodness or bad-
ness of what is sought. After all, if the central institutions
of society are no longer capable of making moral judg-
ments, how should we expect individuals to do so? Take
new techniques of reproduction as an example. Some
couples are sterile, for whatever reason. Before they would
have gone through life without children of their own. Now
they feel they have a right to children, often expressed as a
right to the experience of being a parent, and since the
technology of test tube babies and surrogate mothers is
there to make that possible, how could anyone in his or
her right mind oppose it? Who is society and who is the
next person to presume to impose his or her views on
these deprived people and tell them no? In the name of
what? In the name, perhaps, of the morally dubious quality
of such forms of reproduction? Of old-fashioned ideas of
what it means to be a parent? In the name of the sanctity
of the body and the natural bond between child and
mother? In the name of the envelope of the flesh? Thus do
rights become a mask for the interests of one more social
group, a way to dress up the technically feasible in what
still remains of the moral language of modernity. But the
impetus behind this new development is the convergence

of scientific research with the political capacity of this social group to get its message across and accepted. The public becomes an arbiter in a vast Oprah show, and in true post-modern fashion consults experts to make a decision. Strikes a royal commission, perhaps. Seeks counsel from ethicists, since now the moral dilemmas which humans have had to face for millenniums have become one more domain of expertise.

Individuals, like organizations, like the society itself, clamour for their rights until we wind up strangling on them. Big business versus labour, parents versus kids, individual versus collective, smokers versus non-smokers: it is a form of regulated civil war, where we have forgotten what rights are all about without yet knowing how to talk about contemporary matters in appropriate language. Still being human beings, not knowing how to talk also means not knowing how to act. That is a major problem. In fact, it is *the* problem of post-modern society. Having replaced normative behaviour with procedural regulation, turning questions of life and death into matters of feasibility, rational decision-making, operational management, the society finds itself at a loss when forced to confront questions that are normative to the core. Like giving yourself a constitution. Like trying to decide what it is that forms the basic contours of a society. How to live together with many differences. What happened at Charlottetown the second time around.

4

ONCE THE ACCORD WAS MADE PUBLIC, the political actors staked out their positions. There was something definitely wrong with the picture that emerged. On one side you had Pierre Trudeau, Preston Manning, Jacques Parizeau, Judy Rebick, Deborah Coyne, Gérald Larose, Billy Two Rivers, Lucien Bouchard. On the other side Brian Mulroney, Robert Bourassa, Clyde Wells, Bob Rae, Audrey McLaughlin, Jean Chrétien, Ovide Mercredi, Guy Lafleur. It was almost like an all-star game, with Céline Dion at centre ice singing some version of *O Canada*. Ms. Rebick explained the anomalous lineups by saying that referendums make for strange bedfellows, a word intended in that context to apply to both sexes. I think it was more than simply a case of the referendums. It was *this* referendum, post-modern to the hilt.

The political spectrum of modernity is divided up fairly neatly: left versus right, good versus bad, the oppressed against their oppressors. In post-modernity, the rhetoric of progressive versus reactionary is still there, but the reality is quite different. People and groups who, in the earlier period, would seem like natural allies now wind up on opposite sides of the barricades, while erstwhile enemies are objectively in cahoots. In the great Canadian constitutional debate of 1992 we had separatists and federalists, women's rights activists and defenders of the traditional division of sex roles all on the same side. Ranged against them were the leaders of the three political parties, the head of Canada's Assembly of First Nations, big business, the premiers of Ontario and Québec. Within the population the divisions were just as bizarre. Whatever way one voted, one felt one was betraying some cherished belief. It was not only the people who voted yes who felt as if they were holding their noses.

A good deal of the confusion stems from the failure to recognize the changed terrain on which we have to work out our political differences. When the state is strong, defends the interests of a dominant class in the face of a politically coherent subordinate one, it is easier to understand why the vast majority would tend to be on the attack, slam the state for trying once again to shaft the working man and woman. But we live in an age where the working class is being abolished by capitalism and the state is increasingly fragmented by the multiple clientele groups it tries to satisfy, anticipate, mediate. In the Charlottetown accord, that is exactly what the governments involved tried to do. In the Canada Clause they recognized the rights of Aboriginal peoples to protect their culture and ensure the integrity of their societies; the distinct nature of Québec society; the commitment of Canadians to racial, ethnic and gender equality, to official bilingualism, to the equality and diversity of the provinces. It was probably the most politically correct version of any constitution extant in a western democracy. And to no avail. The document got slammed by the very groups whose rights, to varying degrees, were being enshrined in the constitution.

The criticism itself was interesting. Women's groups opposed the final version because the clause stated only that Canadians were committed to the equality of male and female persons, not that governments were bound by this commitment. They feared that this formulation would have no legal force; on the contrary, it would enable the government to claw back, as they put it, the gains women have already made. They also felt that the Supreme Court was given too much leeway in this accord, a criticism that was echoed by many other opponents. Mr. Parizeau, for example, had no trust in the Charlottetown agreement because too much power was placed in the hands of the judges. Given that the judges always interpret the law, it is interesting that few people in our society have much faith in them. To me it seems indicative of a withering of our faith in the entire political system, in which the courts play a key role. It is as if we suspect, not without foundation, that the courts are going to be asked to arbitrate what we ourselves cannot agree on, one more example of throwing responsibility onto the next guy, and turning the next guy into a fall guy. But there is also another aspect to this distrust, and that is our growing distrust of professionals in general. We mistrust politicians, we mistrust doctors, we mistrust judges. At the drop of a hat we are ready to sue the very people on whose competence we rely. Isn't it strange that although people constantly rank professionals at the top of the occupational ladder, they are highly suspicious of that which they esteem? It is as if we no longer believe in the very texture of our social life, as if the whole edifice rests on a very fragile consensus that can be toppled at any moment.

Even the words are taken to mean the opposite of what is conveyed. It is true that to assert Canadians are committed to gender equality, is not the same thing as saying their governments are. On the other hand, if enshrinement in a constitution is taken as some form of recognition, it is better to mention it than not mention it, for the courts would be confronted with that clause in a way they would not if it were absent. Yet if women's rights were protected by the Charter, then why all the mobilization in the first place?

Women's groups were not the only groups to read the Charlottetown accord that way. Québec nationalists also protested that the Canada Clause did not do what it seemed to have done. True, Québec was recognized as a distinct society, but it was also stated that Canadians confirm the principle of the equality of the provinces. For them too, far too much was left to the courts; and although Québec had received a guarantee of twenty-five per cent representation in the House of Commons whatever happens to its demographic curve, the *indépendantistes* screamed Québec's veto had been abandoned. Of course, as Mr. Parizeau said himself in his television debate with Mr. Bourassa, the real problem is that Mr. Bourassa did not succeed in getting Québec recognized as a nation. Mr. Trudeau, for his part, claimed that the new deal allowed for different levels of governments to trample the rights of individuals. Such would be the result of recognizing Québec as a distinct society; such would also be the result of granting Aboriginal peoples self-government, even though Mr. Trudeau himself favoured self-determination, and even though the accord stipulated that the Charter of Rights and Freedoms would apply to Aboriginal governments.

In short, the Charlottetown provisions included many clauses, some of which may have appeared to contradict others. The net effect, however, was to have ensured that individual rights would be respected, while accommodating what was seen as the legitimate demands and aspirations of different groups and communities that make up the country. Once again, to no avail. In the coalition of forces opposing the deal, there were those who condemned it for caving into collective rights at the expense of individual rights, while others denounced it for not going far enough in recognizing the rights of specific social groups. What actually was happening, in typically post-modern fashion, was that every social actor with an agenda saw fit to push for its members' interests and read the document in that light. Rights were demanded, accorded, disputed, rejected in so far as those who sought to benefit by them felt they would indeed do so. Given that context, it's not surprising the deal got such a bad reception. In a society of permanent mobilization, everybody is on their guard, and it's not for Canada.

One ought, in all fairness to the labouring population, point out that much of this imbroglio was the result of the way our elected leaders went about the whole process.

They dearly wanted some kind of accord, and went about getting one in the only way they knew how. They dealt. Québec versus Alberta. The Aboriginals versus history and public opinion. Multiculturalism versus bilingualism. Collective rights versus individual freedoms. Tory against New Democrat. And so on and so forth, far into the night. Somewhere down the line people forgot this was the constitution, the society's founding document. It required a long historical perspective, some deep philosophical reflection, leadership, statesmanship. It required that politics be raised for once above the level of a brokerage house and merger deals. It required that for real, not simply in the twilight homilies of the Minister for Constitutional Affairs. But a deal was what they came up with; understandably people had problems with it. There was no obvious coherence, no fundamental founding principles. It was an attempt to please as many of the most vocal groups as possible, the ones with real political clout. Hence the descending scale of commitments. Hence too the concerns of people that too much was left to future arbitration, and the arbitration would be chancy, dependent on how much bargaining power the different actors involved would be able to exercise. The end result was a massive no, from coast to coast, and a further erosion in the political life of the society. Mr. Clark worried aloud about that. He may have been more right than he knew.

5

AFTER THE REFERENDUM HAD TURNED IN its verdict, I heard an American expert on something or another interviewed on the radio. He was amazed at the result. He was also worried, for he saw right away that if Canada could not come to some measure of agreement about its differences, what hope was there for the rest of the nations? After all, our differences, relatively speaking, were not soaked in blood, and our circumstances were not the most straitened in the world. More than that, though, he understood that the context was much the same as exists in the United States, France, Germany. Here, after all, was an agreement between the federal government, ten provincial premiers, and the leader of the Aboriginal peoples; concluded after months and months of negotiations, public conferences, commissions, discussions; whose overall orientation was to commit the society, sometimes abstractly, sometimes concretely, to the recognition of its major components in line with principles of individual equality and yet redress some glaring historical wrongs. The outcome was failure, democratically arrived at. The man must have been wondering what would happen to his own country if it had to decide on a constitution today. The Canadian experience would seem like Laura Secord candy.

All things considered, we had four basic interest groups: Québec, the West, the Aboriginals, and women. If the same exercise were conducted south of the border, that number would have jumped to twenty-five. Next time round, we won't get off so easily either. Already some of the women's groups' spokespersons were rejecting the accord because it didn't make any provision for gay rights.

And wait until kids get into the act, not to mention foetuses, the visually challenged, criminals and their victims; the list of particular rights goes on and on, expanding with the system. Which raises a crucial issue: how can we make people feel at home, give to those who have felt disenfranchised, snubbed, discriminated against for so long, the security that they can act as full citizens, without founding the social order on the fragmentation which comes from turning difference into rights? In a democracy subordinate groups feel entitled, and they are; but to what? No woman should be denied a job because she is a woman, paid less because she is a woman, left uneducated because she is a woman. No man should be beaten up because he sleeps with another man. No child should be abused because he or she is a child. These are simple precepts, aren't they? Do they have all to be enumerated in a constitution?

When Arendt discussed the French Revolution, she suggested it failed because its leaders tried to settle a social question with political means when the solution was technical and, at that point in time, beyond their means. There was no way they could legislate the poverty of the *sans-culottes* out of existence. They simply had to wait for a century of economic development. In post-modern society, the situation is somewhat similar, but we have carried the process a step further. We want to get rid of the political means altogether and treat political questions as technical ones, as problems of social engineering. It is a recipe for disaster, a spiral into confusion. Maybe that's why the Charlottetown agreement only committed Canadians to gender equality. Perhaps stating the broad principle is enough for starters, for one can easily imagine a process of endless litigation, where every situation is scrutinized for how well it measures up to the formal principle. One quickly winds up with the situation at my university regarding equal access to jobs: questionnaires, policies, committees, studies, the panoply of experts ready to move in and create more problems in search of a solution. Some things do settle themselves in time. Some things don't. But that's life. Do we have to pulverize a society in order to do what ought to be done anyway?

I know. People will say what ought to be done should have been done long ago. For thousands of years it has been said: feed the hungry, clothe the naked, give shelter to those without. Perhaps people have, within their means. It is only with the advent of industrial society that we have begun to think what was a moral obligation has become a right. And we have grafted onto that another notion of rights, as people have come to reject what also has been said for thousands of years: keep the woman at home, stone the homosexual; or for hundreds: carry the white man's burden. That something has slowly changed in the consciousness of humanity so that today we reprove what earlier epochs endorsed, does not necessarily mean that the way to accomplish our new set of values is simply to stand the past on its head.

The doctrine of rights is a tricky business. It emerged in the context of the modern state as part of its universalizing tendency. Citizens had rights because the government was founded on the consent of its citizens. If sovereignty was not lodged in the king, it had to lodge in the people. But the rights were universal rights, the ones people had as human beings endowed with the universal capacity of reason, guaranteeing them protection from the arbitrary rule of the state, monarchical or otherwise. They were not particular rights accorded to people by virtue of their status in society. That came later, as corporations became legal persons and the working class clamoured for its social rights. In the wake of these developments, movements for rights of all kinds flourished. But these later, particular rights should not be confused with individual rights. The latter carried with them a host of duties, as the French Declaration of the Rights of Man amply makes clear. These duties were duties to the nation, in tacit recognition that rights of this nature were bound up with the political community that conferred them. The transition from individual to particular rights, is the transition from modern to post-modern society. The recognition of these latter-day rights is sought in terms of emancipation from the political community. Indeed, in the long run, their ultimate satisfaction implies what Marx once dreamed about: the withering away of the state.

The process is worth exploring, if only because it is not self-evident. The demands of particular groups in today's society partly refer to rights in the classical sense. Having suffered different forms of oppression or exclusion, they find that the universal ideals of bourgeois society were insufficient to give them the protection which they promised. Asking for recognition of their rights by virtue of their status, is seen as a necessary way to force society to do for them what it does for its privileged members. Women, gays, children, blacks are thereby only demanding their human rights, the ones linked to a political community. At the same time these rights become quickly transformed into a confirmation of their social status and an arm to enable them to enhance it. The pursuit of these particular rights is used to force courts, enterprises, organizations to modify social practices and redistribute social resources like jobs, pay, goods, forms of care. In the course of these pursuits different groups get pitted against one another, sometimes in alliance with and sometimes in opposition to the state itself. Conflict increases. Experts are called in to regulate the disputes. Complexity waxes. Confusion is usually not far behind.

In the Charlottetown accord the confusion was fairly evident. Some opponents of the accord were in favour of individual rights but against collective rights, such as those ceded to Québec or to Aboriginal governments. Many who were in favour of individual rights had no qualms equating them with particular rights of definite social categories, like female persons or the ethnic and racial groups to whose equality Canadians were also committed. Then there was the Reform Party, on record as being against multiculturalism although it is in favour of equal opportunity for all Canadians regardless of race or creed. And the Parti Québécois; in favour of collective rights and individual rights, but only within an independent Québec. And of course, the federal government and the signatories to the document, who were in favour of all three: individual rights, collective rights, and particular rights. No problem. No contradiction. Post-modernism at its finest. Let's be practical.

The funny thing is, as sophisticated and technical as post-modern organization is, it's often anything but practical. Questions which seem fairly clear quickly become rather complicated, as often happens when you don't think things through. It ought to be apparent by now that the discussion of the Canadian constitution cannot be held solely in terms of rights, and certainly not as that doctrine is now used. Hard as it may be to believe, the recourse to rights will only serve to sink us deeper into the quagmire. There are rights that are important to preserve, but there are other things that are important to preserve that are not rights, and do not need the status of rights in order for us to preserve them. A country, for example. A past, for another. A future, for a third. Then there are things we might want to do that concern not so much preserving as redressing: historical wrongs, or recognizing: a founding people. We also might want to get our vocabulary clear, so we will know how to talk about these matters without feeling beholden to positions that make no sense.

6

LET'S GO BACK TO THE BEGINNING, since that's what constitutions are all about. When Mr. Mulroney was first elected Prime Minister, he promised to get Québec to sign the Canadian constitution. He thought it was important for Canadian unity, perhaps because he himself came from Québec. Surely a not unworthy goal. The first attempt at achieving this aim resulted in the Meech Lake accord, which went the way of all flesh. The second was the Charlottetown agreement, dubiously entitled the Canada round. There we found out that the children's verse about sticks and stones is not so true. Names can hurt you, at least when you no longer worry about broken bones.

So there was the problem of Québec, the perennial problem, which ought to tell us something about its distinctness. Does Manitoba provoke constitutional crises? It did once, but settled it in rather high-handed fashion, rewriting the terms of its entry into Confederation by transforming its status as a bilingual province into a unilingual English one. Today it tries to give lessons to Québec about the importance of respecting minority rights. Another old story we tell to children, this one about the pot calling the kettle black.

Why is it so difficult to tell things as they are? Is it a failing particular to post-modern times, or only more noticeable? It probably doesn't take a genius to recognize that Québec is somehow different from the rest of Canada, if only by the fact that people here speak French. Is that grounds for turning it into an independent state? Hardly, one might answer; but that does not mean that Québec is a province like the others. The separatist forces in Québec like to argue that because Québec is different it has rights, like the right to self-determination. They also like to argue that because Québec is oppressed, it has rights. It may, however, be that Québec is simply Québec, a product of history with a certain number of concerns, one of which is that if something is not done, French will disappear on the North American continent. The concern is not un-reasonable. It ought really to be a Canadian concern, at least if we value difference.

Does Québec have rights? Not really. It has powers, which is much more important, guaranteed by the BNA Act, and like any good post-modern actor, it would like more. A good deal of the constitutional wrangling was all about that: who gets what and how much and at whose ex-pense. In that respect Québec was not alone. Every actor in the drama wanted more, just like Oliver Twist with his bowl of soup. Rights became a code word for not having to say please. And the welter of conflicting rights became the pretext for saying no. But the problem will not go away, just as women will not quietly go home, nor gays return to the closet. What to do, since the hour is decidedly blue?

For one, we might separate the discussion of difference from the discussion of rights. Two, we might examine our history to see what has made us, the good and the bad, before deciding what it is we would like to put right. Three, we might choose to put reasonable limits on what we can do and not do. Modest proposals to start with, distinctly unpost-modern.

Some people would argue it's an exercise in futility. Politics is basically a struggle for power, always is and al-ways has been. Québec and the federal government slug it out, in order to see how much each can get. Mr. Trudeau accused all Québec governments in recent memory of having practised a form of profitable federalism, and in many respects they have. But so too have the other provin-ces. When the West complains about the cost of bilin-gualism, are they not doing much the same? When British

Columbia was up in arms about the deal because its demographic weight was not being recognized, wasn't that also a way of saying: politics is numbers, wealth, and in Canada a warm climate, let's have that translated into power? When the federal government tried to sell the deal on the grounds that to reject it would be economic curtains, wasn't it limiting politics to a form of bludgeoning? All of this is undoubtedly true, but it is not the whole story. If it is, and indeed many of our élites operate as if it is, then the final lesson of history is that the most lucid form of political behaviour is one based on sheer force. That indeed is what the post-modern result of five centuries of political scrutiny has yielded, as political science and political practice, all the prattle about pluralism and democracy notwithstanding. One has only to listen to the inside dope, the hard-biting analysis of after the fact commentary and its mercifully more humorous version on the Royal Canadian Air Farce. But in actual fact, human beings find it difficult to live by power alone. That's what raises them one cut above blind instinct. They are moved by something outside themselves, moved to reflection and moved to charity. Perhaps that too is why the country voted no on Charlottetown. Perhaps the people know that the country is integrated from coast to coast, tied by economics and history, obliged to divide up powers in one way or another; but refuse to reduce the question of the country and its foundations to the pragmatic distribution of the interests of governments and the people who would run them, and even of the people for whom they stand. This would make the people less post-modern than their handlers, a possibility one ought to be wary of and yet entertain. It reminds us of the up side of existence, and the reason we take pains to reflect and debate on questions such as our common future.

In the case of the Québec-English Canada imbroglio that launched this recent round of constitutional negotiations, this caveat would remind us that the nationalist position strikes a chord in the Québec population that goes beyond the more narrow interests of the élite that founded the Parti Québécois. It even goes beyond the now bankrupt position of the *souverainistes*. Once, the project of Québec independence was draped in the Third World rhetoric of throwing off the chains of colonialism and imperialism. Now that it has received the benediction of an indigenous economic élite, the rhetoric has shifted into post-modern gear: we will achieve independence because we can do it, and because we can do it, it's worth doing. Thirty years of discourse has turned an aspiration into fact, at least fact of some kind. Many of the next generation of Québécois take independence for granted, not as something requiring justification, even though they are aware that it comes with no *projet de société* attached. When you push a little, you find that they are worried about what will happen to the French language. That it, like other modern languages, is going down the tubes in a school system that doesn't know what education means — another small price to pay for post-modern progress — does little to change the thinking about independence. When you push a little more, you come up against two centuries of resentment, little trust that *les anglais* can be counted on to protect the French language. One starts to hear the litany: the deportation of the Acadians, the hanging of Louis Riel, the chicanery of the West in abolishing French, the difficulty of finding French cab drivers in Ottawa or seeing bilingual gas coupons in Ontario. And yes, you think it's all true, down to Don Getty's musings about the need to abolish what little there is of bilingualism.

Perhaps everybody in this country hates each other, at best is indifferent to the next social group over. That too, after all, is a time-worn human custom. Perhaps that junk in the proposed constitution about racial and ethnic equality was only the pure ideology it reads like. Fifty years after the Wannsee Conference we still haven't learned that the only race around is the human race, still haven't learned to talk properly at the highest levels of society. If we think there should not be discrimination on the basis of skin colour, why don't we simply say so instead of upgrading skin colour to the status of race? Post-modern society has a funny way of talking that pays little attention to words. No wonder the language is doing poorly. Have you noticed how people are now human resources? Even directors of personnel are out. And what, pray tell, is an ethnic group? Is it a word for race when people are embarrassed to use the word race? Is it a word for religion in an age when religion is out? Perhaps it's a substitute for culture in a society that confuses culture with cuisine. In the same clause of the Charlottetown accord where Canadians were committed to racial and ethnic equality, it was stated that Canada is a society built by citizens from many lands, which explains why the clause also refers to the Canada they built as one that reflects its cultural and racial diversity. This presumably is the Canadian way of thanking the impressed Chinese railroad gangs who helped Sir John A. MacDonald tie us sea to sea. More than that, however, it is a masterpiece of semantic confusion, for it ties ethnic group to race, culture, and country of origin without including those two founding peoples whose denomination we try to avoid. They have another role, that gets us into a different kind of hot water.

Ethnicity must be one of the most confusing categories in post-modern society. My sense is it is a catch-all term, multi-functional as the technocrats like to say. On the one hand, it serves as a reference point for identity in a world which gives people a false sense of who they are. In modern society you were a citizen. If you thought modern society was a class society, you were a worker more often than nought. In post-modern society you are a person in search of yourself, on a journey of self-realization. See how far we have come from the olden days, when everyone was a child of God. But that's what happens when the central social institutions no longer secrete transcendent norms.

You too become the sum of your parts, and always after the fact. It's not an easy situation, which is why people indulge in so much therapy, always reconstructing the self. In such a world of disarray, ethnicity helps. It gives a sense of identity, one among others, without being overly strong. It's like religion, without being religion. It's like skin colour, without being that; shades into visible minority although it can be invisible. And it's like culture understood as folklore, weak national tradition done up in restored open-air urban markets, preferably down by a waterfront. It's country of origin without the nation. And in post-modern societies with considerable immigration, it can be an effective strategy for upward social mobility.

This is convenient for groups, who can demand rights, policy measures, employment opportunities on criteria of ethnicity. It is also convenient for governments, who use ethnic diversity as a sign of their openness, tolerance, pluralism. For all the actors concerned, it means they can go on behaving in typically post-modern fashion without having to think seriously about questions like identity or democracy, since the answers are given by practice, by the way things work. Ethnicity might be a problematical category, but not when it is operationally defined. Then everyone knows what it means, all the code words notwithstanding. What suffers in the process is what it really means to be a human being, and how that makes itself felt in our day and age. What also suffers on occasion is what happens to people in the real world, since many of the policies worked out in response to ethnic politics do not have the intended effect. People still suffer discrimination. And whether Sikhs can wear turbans in the RCMP becomes a question of fundamental rights debated in bars across the country. It sometimes even happens, when people have to decide on a constitution, that the inclusion of provisions for ethnic equality sow even greater confusion.

I can still remember Premier Filmon of Manitoba explaining to the country around Meech Lake that we are
heading for a multicultural future. Aside from a well-or-
ganized Ukrainian community in Manitoba, which the
Premier must feel he has to placate for electoral reasons,
does he really believe that a nation, as a political community, can be conjured up by adding together all the different ethnic groups defined by their country of origin, or
by that of their great-great-grandparents? Does the Ukraine
do that for its expatriate Canadians? Yes, Canada is a
country of immigration, and yes, we live in a world where
the flux of migration is on the increase, slightly behind the
flows of capital. Does that mean that our political defini-
tions have to fall in line, bulldozed by the facts? Is the
political foundation of the society to be confused with the
job prospects of Sri Lankan and Haitian immigrants to
Canada? What about the strategic use of multiculturalism
to deny the historically specific status of Québec, and
beyond it of the French-Canadian people, as one of the
founding peoples of Canada? Can one fact bomb another?
For it is a fact that the Canadian Confederation was put
together between Upper and Lower Canada, between the
English and the French, at the historic encounter in Charlottetown, 1864. Subsequent additions, the creation of new
provinces, an influx of people from the world over cannot
modify that original sin. And like people everywhere, we
shall have to deal with our original sin.

7

IT MAY BE THAT THE LOOSE USE OF TERMS like ethnic and racial serves to obscure the less palatable dimensions of human congregation, here as elsewhere. Laudable as was the apparent aim of going on record by committing Canadians to ethnic and cultural diversity, it is hard to avoid the impression that we are not thus committed. Why were there riots by blacks in Toronto reminiscent of the outrage in L.A.? Why are blacks shot by the police in Montréal all too often in circumstances that leave the impression of racism? It would seem we were about to enshrine in the constitution what we do not have in our streets. It was not going to help the streets, and it was not going to help the constitution. And then again, if we are that committed to diversity, how can Canadians have so much trouble recognizing that Québec is a distinct society?

Some would say that the answer lies in the difference between recognizing that the country includes citizens of different national origins and recognizing that one of the provinces in the federal system is a distinct society. A province means a government, and a government has powers, can use those powers to dump on others by invoking its special status. True enough, although it is worth remembering that there is a Charter of Rights and Freedoms to counterbalance that possibility. It is also worth remembering that this Charter has a notwithstanding clause which enables any Canadian government to override its guaranteed liberties; a far greater danger when you think of it than stating in the constitution that Québec constitutes a distinct society. There is nonetheless a difference, and it resides in the fact that the government is a political body while an ethnic group is not. Not yet, that is, although under post-modern conditions, it, like so many other interest groups clamouring for recognition on the basis of some form of identity, contributes to the weakening of the government's capacity to act in the name of all the citizens, as the embodiment of Rousseau's general will. Something all governments, classical liberal governments, did. That is why ethnic diversity winds up being at loggerheads with the distinct society clause for Québec. They are two fundamentally different notions working in opposite directions. The idea of a distinct society implies a political conception of identity emerging from a political community with some idea of a common purpose. Ethnic diversity, on the other hand, implies that the aim of politics is to manage things in order to allow the multiple forms of identity to express themselves in non-political ways.

Most people wind up identifying with the multicultural approach because it is in conformity with the logic of contemporary society, one variant of what they see as the purpose of living together: to maximize everyone's autonomy. Self-autonomy, one is tempted to write, in order to underline the point. It is as though political action, the humanizing of the world through deliberation and decision in concert with other people, becomes oriented to setting people free of the world. Freedom becomes, as Janis Joplin sang, "just another word for nothing left to lose." Talk about cynicism, a woman once told me.

But there is another aspect to many Canadians' objection to recognizing Québec as a distinct society. It stems not from political considerations, but from an incapacity to see what is distinct about Québec. One hears this objection even in anglophone circles in Montréal. What is distinct about Québec in a way that does not make Manitoba distinct, or Newfoundland, or Saskatchewan, home of medicare? Indeed, when you think about it, we are all distinct, every province, every group, every person, in some way or other. Are we going to put them all in the constitution? This objection runs every difference into one, confounds political ones at the level of a society with sectoral and individual ones within the society, until political distinctions become meaningless and society the outcome of all our differences. If that's what Canada is, little wonder there's no national crowd symbol. Perhaps an equation of infinite regression would do in its stead.

Fortunately or unfortunately, Québec doesn't see itself like that. Its members, francophone but also others, are aware that it exists as a collective entity, but like everyone else, they too have trouble translating that into political terms. Except the *indépendantistes*, who translate it into sovereignty. That's a neat way of resolving the problem, except for the fact that it's not quite clear to many people, including many Québécois, why the sense of being a distinct collective entity merits an independent state. In attempting to justify it, the nationalist groups fall into the same discourse as the rest of Canada. Québec too has rights, collective rights, those belonging to the biggest ethnic group of all, a nation. When people ask: which nation?, the answer implicitly comes back: the French-Canadian nation. Only the French-Canadian nation is scattered across Canada. It is the history of demographics, and the reneged commitments of Canada concerning the status of French in those provinces admitted into Confederation after 1867, that have made Québec to all intents and purposes the inheritor of the French-Canadian nation. This has happened at a time when Québec itself has become a highly immigrant society, reproducing within its borders the same kind of group pressures that surround the multicultural discourse in Canada. The Québec government's Ministry of Cultural Communities is a beehive of the same bizarre paradoxes that littered the Charlottetown accord.

As a collective entity with governmental powers, the Québec government has a responsibility to integrate new immigrants. In post-modern democracies, integration does not mean assimilation, so the government takes pains, at least formally, to pursue a policy of promoting cultural diversity understood as ethnicity. This works against the solidification of a distinct national consciousness. Indeed, the *péquistes* see the ethnic groups labelled allophones as basically hostile to independence. Yet their goal of independence is no longer presented in terms of the French-Canadian nation, since that is an ethnic as opposed to a political definition of the nation. The more they define the Québec state in terms of a civic culture marked by pluralism, especially ethnic, the weaker their claim to a distinct society as the basis of their demand for sovereignty. Some people would even play this paradox against the demand for recognition of a distinct society within Canada. They are, as the saying goes, hoisted with their own petard.

It is, of course, hard to have your cake and eat it, although everybody tries. The irony is that Québec's difficulties are the same as Canada's. The more it tries to have a loose, functional definition of its political community, the less distinct it gets. The more it relies on a hard-core definition of what constitutes the Québec nation, the more it paints itself into an ethnic corner from which it prides itself it has escaped. One way out has been to shift the debate from the terrain of ethnicity to that of rights and language, which is merely to reproduce it in another form.

Québec asserts it has collective rights. Sometimes those rights refer to a common past and tradition, even though that tradition has less and less resonance even for Québécois of old stock. More often than not, they are invoked to defend the French fact, and especially the French language, which is seen to be under attack on the North American continent. The perception is not crazy if one looks at the census figures on language within the borders of NAFTA. When the defense of the French language, however, is joined to the notion of collective rights, the whole whirlpool of the different kinds of rights gets reactivated.

Efforts to defend the French language by politically institutional means are then opposed by people claiming individual rights. Should Québec ever achieve independence, it will have a real problem on its hands, for then all the minority groups will start to demand their rights. Schools, for example, to support ethnic pluralism. The figures on language in North America will not have changed, but a sovereign government will no longer be able to plead its collective rights as an oppressed minority. As a sovereign government it will be the boss, having to deal with the collective rights of minorities within its boundaries. The scenario makes even the current impasse look good.

But not that good. As we trip up over our own language and fall into the quagmire of a political discourse that winds up being the mask for extortionist politics, we reduce the questions of our common existence to the level of resentment and the hurling of insults. In the end, being distinct is a function simply of not being like the next person or group. Being distinct is being the wronged party, and history is turned into a litany of complaints which the present situation can quickly inflame. One reads in newspapers, sees on television, overhears in health club locker rooms the lengthy narratives of jilted lovers. Did you see how they stamped on the *fleur de lys* in Brockville? Did you hear how Sault Ste. Marie voted to make the city unilingually English? The real problem is that without Québec, the ROC would quickly melt into the USA. And on the other side: what does Québec really want? If they're so distinct, how come they vote for free trade and run down to Florida all the time? They have another thing coming if they think the Americans will do half of what we do for the French language. And so it goes, until someone from ROC raises money to put up billboards in Québec saying the Rest of Canada loves you. I suppose it is the appropriate response to the shrinking of the public sphere to the psychological domain. But that too is post-modernity, and Canada is very fertile ground. We seem to be caught in

some *film noir* variant of Buber's I and Thou, playing at
our national pastime of acceptance and rejection, some interminable love affair whose major refrain, as in all love affairs, is you don't love me enough. I guess it's
understandable. Love is a rare commodity in the world,
and all the more so when it's a substitute for politics.

Perhaps what I am getting at is that we do have a few
problems to settle, but not all the problems are of the same
order and not all require constitutional enshrinement. The
difficulties we had in settling our constitutional hash are
the same that make it so difficult to treat certain questions
for what they are. It should not be that difficult to protect
the French language in Québec, perhaps even to promote
it, if we could discuss that issue freely in all its parameters,
and not as an instrument for or against sovereignty, nor as
a litmus test for human rights. Indeed, if we could agree
about which country we wanted to be in, and under what
broad terms, if we could agree on what it means to have a
country today, perhaps people would be slightly more
reasonable.

8

L ET'S LOOK FOR A MOMENT at the precarious status of the French language. Not in the world, not in the new edition of Proust, not in *la France éternelle* with its lovely Provence and *foie gras* and champagne in supermarkets, but here in this rude corner of the world, where temperature drops to minus twenty-four celsius and despite the wonders of Hydro-Québec and Alberta's oil and natural gas, we still imagine we are a bunch of *voyageurs* preserving the wonders of a dictionary in the face of an ice age or the lazy appeal of blueberries in summer.

Viewed within the narrow confines of Canadian history, the status of French has progressively shrunk. There were once thriving French-speaking communities from coast to coast. The country was indeed bilingual, certainly more so than it is today, and was recognized as such in our formal political arrangements. In 1890 the government of Manitoba adopted a law making English the only official language in that province and suppressing the Catholic French schools of the Franco-Manitobans. That Gabrielle Roy became the accomplished writer she was, owed nothing to the benign eye of her native Manitoba. At the same time, the federal government supported a bill allowing the future provinces of Alberta and Saskatchewan, still grouped together in the North-West Territories, to choose the language of their debates and publications. The Assembly in the Territories henceforth had a free hand to use the weight of its English population, far superior numerically, to withdraw from French its status of an official language. It took one citizen's challenge of a parking ticket a century later for the Supreme Court to declare the whole process unconstitutional.

By then, however, the damage had been done. After the initial push of the Rule Britannia forces, the facts had been left to speak for themselves. Today the leaders of the Western provinces quite understandably can't understand what the fuss is all about. Nor can far too many of their constituents. Bilingualism is seen as costly and a way to take away civil service jobs from people who are entitled to them. It is one more instance of Central Canadian dominance, Québec this time instead of Ontario. Leaning on the facts, they even feel that it is a denial of individual rights. As the Reform Party explains its stance on bilingualism: they are for freedom of speech, opposed to comprehensive language legislation, although in no way do they discourage personal bilingualism. As if every decision about what language the government's laws were to be issued in, or what was to be the *lingua franca* of a country, were simply a matter of personal choice. Canada: the country of exile after the tower of Babel. Like good postmodernists, the Reformers know how to dress up their language to support what it is they want to do anyway, confident that politics is the art of winning power and managing the system's unfolding dynamic. I know that to some, the Reform Party seems like a group dedicated to turning back the clock. Which they are in many ways, but all their clocks are quartz, and so they too are doomed to the times. Besides, if the Reform Party is deemed reactionary, does that make former Premier Getty and the Conservatives progressive? Mr. Getty was, after all, the man who tried to explain the Reform Party position, when he said that Westerners, like all Canadians, are in favour of bilingualism, they just didn't want it shoved down their throats. Last time I looked, Canadians speaking the other national language naturally had their mouths open, but an accent hardly looked like a tongue depressor.

One can begin to understand why Québécois feel they live under siege. One can also understand why the English community in Québec never talks about what has happened to French outside it. It exhibits a certain historical amnesia so typical of this country, and so convenient when this group advances its cause, reproducing within the confines of Québec the drama that has already gone on outside. The English community in Québec tries to defend its institutions by claiming its rights. Collective rights, one might add, that are really powers, privileges, guarantees, written into the BNA Act. But perhaps, unconsciously, Québec's anglos remember that such safety nets were of little use to French-Canadians out West and mobilize to kick up a fuss before it is too late for them. No doubt, as well, they watch their declining numbers as people head down the 401 and worry that the facts will resolve the political question. By the time a compromise is reached, they risk being a group of rights in search of a community.

On the other foot, the shoe does not fit that much better. French is definitely a minority language on this continent. Turning Québec into a separate state will not change that fact of life. Nor is it that clear that Québec independence will do much to promote or defend the French language in Québec, unless people sincerely believe that it is a declining anglophone community that is blocking its development. Indeed, there are times when I wonder how concerned most Québécois are about their language, as they and I watch it slide downhill, and how much the defense of the French language is a rallying cry to legitimate what another élite group would like to do: get their paws on the Québec state to an even greater degree. Not only the self-avowed separatists, but the managerial class right across the board: union presidents, chairmen of industries, deputy ministers, members of federalist political parties who prepare reports that ask for powers in every area because, when you get down to it, everything is language. Allaire asked for everything, kitchen sink included.

The Arpin report, which was a document on Québec culture, never once stopped to reflect what culture was, took it for granted, in typical post-modern fashion, that culture was what was produced and consumed as such, got prizes, boosted revenues. *Le déclin de l'empire américain. Un zoo la nuit.* Culture was what the artistic milieu said was culture and the artistic milieu was what got government grants. Exit Baudelaire, Réjean Ducharme, Marie-Claire Blais. Enter a new distribution of powers, to be negotiated in cultural agreements after Charlottetown was approved. But the graduates of our community colleges, like those everywhere else, can barely put a complete sentence together. You know. Whatever. Just try and use the subjunctive in the imperfect tense. Try and hear it used in the National Assembly. On television. In daily conversation. It's too long for a sound byte. And then there are the universities, where people trained in elegant French let students pass their courses with high marks, alleging that bad grammar and faulty syntax do not hinder the comprehension of a text. The students wonder why marks should be given for the quality of French, are even outraged at this denial of their rights. What rights, you wonder, aside from the desire to get a diploma for doing time. But they too tend to be for independence. In order to protect the French language. Maybe they are thinking of future generations.

It might be, however, that despite the poor historical record, Canada is the best protection for French. A bilingual Canada, that is, not the sloppy version we have now. I know people think it is impractical. Both the Reform Party and the Parti Québécois would nix the idea, claiming rights, facts, the wrongs of the past, not to mention the high costs, the waste of resources, the absurdity of forced-feeding. Besides, they say, it's been tried, and point to the Official Languages Act. I remember visiting The Rocks in New Brunswick, this strange promontory that goes down to the Moncton River as it widens into the Bay of Fundy. At the bottom there are these enormous bonsai plants, gardens atop immense rocks, free-standing caves carved out of the cliffs by the ancient wear of the Earth's heavings. The river is the colour of iron and the weight of human labour. It is all too incredible, like God holding back the walls of the Red Sea so the Israelites could pass through in safety. And this bit of wonder belongs to Canada, in a manner of speaking. At the top explanations are spelled out, as is the wont in national parks, in both official languages; but the French version is full of mistakes. I reported it to one of the students working there for the summer. I wonder if they have been rectified. In a bilingual Canada that wouldn't happen. Shouldn't.

But in a post-modern society people don't like to talk about should and shouldn't. They like to be practical, like Preston Manning and Jacques Parizeau. Only, not everything in life is a question of costs and not all costs are costly. As people have often pointed out apropos of Québec's demand for increased powers in order to avoid duplication, not every joint jurisdiction is wasteful; in some, dollars are even more wisely spent. But the question of a bilingual Canada is not a question of money, cannot be decided on the grounds of how many jobs it will create or take away, how much upward or downward mobility it will engender. Not even on the grounds of the latest pedagogical theories about whether a child has first to master one language. It is a question of the kind of country we want. If we think this country was put together by two founding peoples — yes, two, because it is not certain that the Iroquois Confederacy would have produced this version of Canada — then we ought to recognize that fact in our basic institutions and laws. We even ought to cherish it. It's part of our history, what made us who we are. I presume I am not the only one who thinks like that, since the French immersion schools across the country are bursting at their seams.

It won't work, people will say. The country is too big. A language is a living thing, needs a real context to grow in. If people don't use it, see no need to use it, it will wither and die. Maybe, but maybe the reverse will happen. People will exchange electronic mail in two languages, listen to poetry readings without translation. The Prime Minister can deliver a speech without repeating what he said or changing the nuances to suit the linguistic audience. Teachers will have a field day on exchange programs across the country. Students too. Canadians will feel an obligation mixed with pride to speak two languages. They will come to value language for its own sake and strike a blow against post-modernism. In a world full of difference, that each day shrinks into that global village another Canadian described, we would find that it's worth first learning to understand the difference in your own back yard. We might start to get off on some of that other diversity our latter-day fathers of Confederation wanted to enshrine at Charlottetown. Maybe the cops will be less nervous when dealing with suspects whose skin colour falls at the black end of the rainbow. I know that when I hit Vancouver in my car, I'd love to see those traffic signs in French. I'd feel less lonesome for that other language that still remains my second.

It could be, of course, that I have my own axe to grind. I am, after all, an anglo in Québec who teaches at a French university. I have spent a good deal of my life trying to master that language and wonder if it's all for nought. I know I shall never be able to write like Proust in French, while I can continue to dream that in English I shall one day equal Faulkner. I find it hard to return to my native language in a city where most publishing roads lead to Paris. I miss hearing English spoken in the streets. Maybe I'm discouraged and want Canada to come to my rescue. Maybe I should pack up and move to Toronto. Perhaps, like Julien Green, I should really master French. Perhaps I'm lucky to have all these options, even as complaints. Do you see what Canada produces?

There are even days I think that it is silly to want to protect a language. What is the point in the long scheme of things? What can it possibly mean? A language will survive if people use it, love it, create great literature with it. But one day that language too will die out, like the Sumerian language did, and like all languages will as history rolls through time and the sun grows cold. That too is post-modern consciousness; having a very long memory while seeing far enough into the future to know that the planet, as we know it, cannot exist forever. A step beyond Tennyson. But then I think: we live now, not at the end of time. Have to live now, together, trapped in the history that is ours, which of course is part of being human. So it's kind of understandable that French-speaking Québécois would want to protect their language. And there ought to be a way to do it without getting all entangled in a web of conflicting rights and sovereignties. Some things are practical, but in typical post-modern fashion, it is always the most practical tasks that become the most complicated. The simple things, like the simple light, require that extra touch of expertise, the helping hand that makes everything so difficult. Bill 101. The *Conseil du statut de la langue française*. Bill 178. And an English language community that doesn't think it's natural for signs in Québec to be in French. Which brings us back to the basic political problem that we don't really know how willing we all are to embrace this country in both languages. As long as we refuse to commit ourselves, to say, English to French and French to English, that we are equal partners until death do us part, numbers of offspring notwithstanding, and put our constitution where history has led our unacknowledged hearts, we will continue to try and regulate that which cannot be regulated. And find ourselves periodically, as we did last fall at Charlottetown, in a jam of unbelievable proportions. As a character at the end of one of Yehoshua's novels put it, "suddenly you're in a terrible mess".

9

SPEAKING OF MESSES, try self-determination on for size. Self-determination is a concept that manages to combine individual and collective rights without mentioning either. It has a better press than collective rights, since the self makes us think of the individual. It is also the epitome of post-modern politics, since it falls in line with widely held beliefs about the importance of self-realization. Actually, they are not only beliefs, given that more and more people conduct their lives on that basis, treating them like stages or management crises on the way to full accomplishment. But there is something ultimately and deeply false about that notion, which lies in a misunderstanding about the very nature of being.

Rainer Maria Rilke, in one of his more mysterious passages, had the mother of one of his characters once warn him never to stop desiring, but also to recognize that there is no accomplishment in life. By combining the two ideas in the same paragraph, he perhaps meant to suggest that it is pointless to stop desiring, since that is part of our nature; yet it is also pointless to think that what we have to accomplish is ourselves, beings of desire. Indeed, what we have to accomplish lies in the world. In doing that, in whatever object we produce outside ourselves, up to and including the society itself, we leave some part of ourselves. Thus are we objectified, accomplished in the world, but every accomplishment exacts its pound of flesh and spirit, and the more we succeed, the less there is of us. How else could saints do what they did? Or the bourgeois?

The bourgeoisie revolutionized the world, gobbled it up through science and industry, through art and revolution. In their own way they were in love with the world. They wanted to find out its secrets, explore its treasures. Consider modernity as one long voyage of Christopher Columbus. Their eyes were not focused inward, since who they were was already given by the social order in which they lived. They were citizens in a politically defined world, just as their predecessors were socially inscribed in a terrestrial city that mirrored heaven. In neither case did human beings think they had identity crises. Their sense of themselves was given to them by virtue of the society they lived in, since the society itself had some form of pre-ordained unity. True, those societies were once founded, constituted at some original point; but the nature of the resulting constitution was such that its members could turn outward to the world, engage in activity secure that they did not have to constantly ask: who am I? This terrible and highly absurd question is particularly post-modern, emerges in a society which no longer has any pre-established social contract. On the contrary, the social consensus is constantly shifting, the product of all our conflicting and mobilized desires. So too is our sense of self, a continuous product of people in search of themselves. It makes for a very precarious sense of existence. Also for a lot of loneliness. Isn't it strange, as the song says?

One of the strange things is that we live in a society where the inner space of human existence has been opened up as never before. We talk about it, discover it, represent it in art, put it on television, parade it right across the country, stark naked. You'd think the possibilities for discovery were endless and everybody was having a great time. So how come everybody's complaining that they can't find a good lover? Friend? Someone to talk to? Someone to have dinner with once a week? How come so many people are getting divorced because their true selves are not satisfied in a relationship? How come so many people are in therapy in order to learn how to become autonomous and manage their autonomy, when all they want is a good man or woman? Has the barrel of human apples turned more rotten than usual?

It could simply be that we are chasing our tails. When you stop to think about it, it's rather absurd that people should be busy finding themselves. How do you lose yourself other than dying? And even then, we don't really know what goes on, although from where we stand, it doesn't seem like much. Perhaps the presupposition is wrong. Perhaps the trick is not to find yourself, since you're always here. If you need proof, look in the mirror. Ring your neighbour's doorbell. As a good Canadian, you might even try the telephone. Of course, it's hard to turn the trick, since the socially constituted messages around us keep inciting us to do the opposite. If a questionnaire were distributed across the country asking people if they valued autonomy as a goal, I bet the yes vote would be pretty high. It's not surprising, given that autonomy is the major reward for holding a job. That's why people rank professionals so highly; they are the ones with the greatest autonomy, however you want to operationalize that term. Even money, which is what most people think they work for, is only a confirmation of status. After all, if you have a job you can get a credit card and then spend money you don't even have. You can even get a bunch of credit cards and fall heavily into debt, just like the government. Autonomy is a prescription for getting out of control, stepping permanently over the line, and then looking at new ways to control that. It is, as they used to say, a contradiction in terms.

What makes it so self-defeating is that it is an unrealizable state. Individuality emerged in the bourgeois world because the political order permitted and sanctioned it. People had a sense of their person that was independent of the social function they carried out, because social roles were no longer glued to their beings. They could move through the world, in and against it. When individuality became autonomy, the political order changed, weakened, dropped progressively out of the picture. Today nobody thinks in terms of grand utopian projects. They're considered the germs of totalitarianism, understood mainly as the squishing of the individual. Collective behaviour is considered reprehensible, at best unimaginable, in a world dedicated to self-determination. Of course, there is still social interaction, but it is seen as that: interaction not bonds, in which the sovereign element is the self, not the state. The upshot is that people are asked to be the foundation and the measure of their own autonomy, which is well nigh impossible. Until now, at least, humanity has developed forms of social life in which the individual was always, in some way or other, indebted to the world. Society was the representation of that debt; a debt of meaning, which made life worthwhile. Today we are living off the last crumbs of the meaning bequeathed by modernity. In a world given over to autonomy, we rely on the social contract of modern society to supply the framework within which we live. That's why, when we get into trouble, we go back to principles like individual rights. But we want the legacy without the framework, without any framework really, and do not know how to go about building one, since by definition it happens pragmatically, as the sum of our actions. The legacy in the meantime has been slightly modified, to justify all that clamouring for autonomy and all the actions that result. With one self-determination brandished against another, we wind up in the predicament that marked the proposals for Aboriginal self-government.

In the Charlottetown accord it was stipulated that the Constitution would be amended to recognize the inherent right of the Aboriginal peoples to self-government within Canada. This would have made the Aboriginal governments one of three orders of government in the country. Some people had trouble with this, but for quite different reasons. On the one hand, the self-government clause was an attempt to give substance to the recognition of the Aboriginal peoples as distinct societies. The exercise of this right was deemed to safeguard and develop their traditions, cultures, identities, economies, and ensure the development of their lands and resources in line with their values, in order to ensure the integrity of their societies. Some people objected that, once again, we were handing over legal and political power to a people defined essentially as an ethnic group, as a way of life. It was hard to see how that would suffice as a basis for citizenship. The critics of this proposal worried that such a clause would prepare the grounds for Native domination of non-Native persons, for a new form of discrimination or exclusion, since defense of their traditions could often be invoked to deny other Canadians their individual rights, including the right to settle within Aboriginal territories. As if in anticipation of this objection, the Charlottetown accord also had a word about including a provision for non-ethnic governments during the process of negotiation, since all this would have to be worked out in years to come. In that section of the accord it was stated that self-government agreements may provide for self-government institutions open to all residents in a region covered by the agreement. May. To many that was not enough, just as women's groups, including Aboriginal women's groups, claimed the accord discriminated against women, since the traditions self-government was supposed to protect and enhance had different weight according to gender. The accord stipulated that the Charter would apply to Aboriginal governments, which would be one way to counter the differential treatment consecrated by tradition. On the other hand, in a section related to gender equality, it stated that the 1982 Constitution's guarantee that Aboriginal and treaty rights apply equally to male and female persons should be retained. These are treaty rights, not individual rights.

There are, here, obvious conflicts and contradictions. It is indeed hard to use people, tradition, a way of life, as the basis for a political form of government in an age when individuals are clamouring for their rights in order to burst the tradition asunder. In modernity, the nation represented the people pole while the state incarnated the individual or citizen end of the political community. This was fine as long as the political community was more or less homogeneous. When it isn't, contradictions come fast and furious. This is even more so when individual rights are asserted in terms of autonomy, where the self would like to become free of all political bonds. When that happens, self-determination at the individual level, often defined in particularist terms — as membership in a status group with its own identity and need for emancipation — comes into conflict with self-determination defined in collective terms. We assume the political arrangements of modernity in an age where they are crumbling, and deal with the reality we presume in fact but ignore in thought, by resorting to conventions about ethnicity. When the debate breaks out, the presumptions explode in our face. To put it in another way, in our attempt to come to grips with our long-standing relationship to the Aboriginal peoples of this country, post-modernity has caught up with traditional society in an age where modernity is dead. We want somehow to put things right, but we don't quite know how. We lack the political language, just as we lack it for ourselves.

In some ways the Native leaders understand that. Those who opposed the accord took self-government to its logical conclusion, just like the rebellions of 1837 in Upper and Lower Canada. Those Native leaders didn't want self-government within Canada. They wanted recognition as a nation. That's what self-determination is all about, at least in its recent historical formulation in the wave of decolonization that followed the Second World War. The Parti Québécois understands that, which is why its deputies were not so sympathetic to Mr. Mercredi's remarks at a parliamentary hearing in Québec. One distinct society calls forth another. One independence, the next. In the end Mr. Mercredi was willing to settle for self-government within Canada. Many were not and called for a boycott of the referendum. If the whites were going to make amends, that was fine and dandy, but it had nothing to do with them. They did not recognize Canada's sovereignty. That's the running bone of contention with the Mohawks at Khanawake, even if they are selling contraband cigarettes in downtown Montréal. No doubt, that's how a dispute over a golf course at Oka turned into an armed conflict between Mohawks and the Canadian army. Another mess we got out of by the skin of our teeth.

I suppose one day we will all be asking: what do the Indians want? And from there we will move into hyperbole and recrimination, bewildered at our own confusion. The problem, perhaps, is that everyone wants everything. We want to settle all the problems at once and preferably by the same means. What do the Indians want? Land, to start with, the land they have always known. It must have one day been an infinite horizon, land in a generic sense that goes on and on, like this vast mass of rock and pine we call Canada. They also want powers, for without jurisdiction over the land it will be nothing but the reserves we have created; and even that might go the way of all dams. And if they want all that, it must be to try and maintain a way of life distinct from what we have to offer, or they wouldn't need the land at all. They could simply form an investment corporation. Perhaps that's what will happen. Setting up gambling casinos is not exactly the accepted version of the traditional way of life. But if we are going to recognize that the purpose of self-government is to protect a way of life, we might also have to recognize that the forms of traditional society are not those of modernity, let alone of post-modernity. There is something incompatible between individual rights and traditional forms of social behaviour. I remember Mr. Mercredi explaining to a *Cité libre* dinner once that Native government worked by consensus. That to him was the safeguard for the individual. He even ventured to suggest it was more democratic than consulting people once in four years about the leaders they wished to select. He refrained from commenting on the conditions under which our elections are conducted. It sounded nice, but I had trouble imagining how any group I knew of beyond my friends could function by consensus. It was a nice idea because, if implemented, time would slow down, our pace of life change, what we consider important come to assume a different configuration. But it didn't seem in the cards, and I had suspicions about the extent of Native democracy. Yet in a way I didn't care. That was their way of doing things. How important is it that it be called democracy?

The question is not: what do the Indians want, but what do we want? Perhaps we want to redress some historic wrongs. That's already a significant achievement, like getting out of the Oka crisis without a bloodbath. Some people thought Mr. Bourassa was a wimp, didn't come down hard enough to assert Québec sovereignty. I thought just the opposite: it was a miracle for which we ought to thank him. In another country the army would have gone in blazing. The summer was hot, the bridge to Montréal was closed, tempers were rising; and in the background international teams came to inspect human rights abuses. The Canadian way is sometimes very good indeed.

In Charlottetown we wanted to make amends and came up with the idea of Aboriginal governments on land within Canada. It was not really self-determination, but then it's hard to rewrite history completely. There are treaties, pipelines, hydroelectric projects. There is television. There are airplanes. An integrated school system. Alcohol. Dope. We have to make peace with that history too, and the present belongs to it as well. Part of the present includes members within Native societies who are already thinking to the future and so would transform them. Maybe they will, but as we well know from our own institutions that were born in the bosom of traditional society, it is hard to adapt them and keep their meaning. What did he say, Mc-Luhan, about the medium being the message? We cannot simultaneously guarantee the transformation and the preservation. In other words, we cannot give powers to preserve traditional society and at the same time institute a system of rights that will undermine it, not unless the Aboriginal peoples themselves want to work that in too. Perhaps that's why there's need for so much negotiation. At any rate, it's certainly unfair to criticize an agreement for doing what we think it ought to be doing. It's like asking traditional society to be post-modern. You can always ask, I suppose, but one would do best to rely on the forces of history. Even with their self-government, Native peoples would be hard pressed to resist the encroachment of today's social forces. That's what threatens them most of all, if threatens is the right term. Then too, warrior societies also threaten, in a different way.

Perhaps Native peoples occupy a space in our imagination the way Paddle-to-the-Sea does in mine. Perhaps they are our nostalgia for the world we have lost and the image of hope for the world we are stuck in. In some twist of our unconscious, perhaps we suspect that all those words about respecting tradition might one day prove true, that they will find a path out of post-modernity in a way that for us is barred by history. And perhaps we'd like to keep them preserved like autumn vegetables, grateful that some-one, somewhere, in the true north strong and free, is wor-rying about keeping the rivers clean and the land as pristine as we like to think of it. The question of Aboriginal self-government might merely be another way of asking how post-modern we really want Canada to be.

10

THE CHARLOTTETOWN ACCORD TRULY was a post-modern document. Even as I reread it I am struck by how generous all the partners to the deal were. They had something for everyone, for every group in Canada that had some political clout, and not only statements of principles. Often these groups were given real powers. If one reads the thrust of the document, one cannot help but notice that the overall tone is conciliatory, open, democratic, an attempt to include as many differences as possible and assure groups hitherto wronged or subordinate that their grievances would be redressed, their rights assured. These differences, one ought to add, were quite enormous, sometimes cutting across historical epochs. Much was left to future negotiations. Given the nature of the different demands that were addressed, perhaps that is understandable. People did not like that either. Too much was left to the technocrats to work out, which it was; but that too is how post-modernity functions. The satisfaction of so many demands turns politics into management, and management requires constant elaboration, modification, adjustment, in line with the inputs into the system and the feedback they create. In an odd way, although the document was very politically correct, it was not a political document. Hence the widespread dissatisfaction; and yet it was not so easy to oppose, since it seemed we were rejecting measures that seemed progressive. Mr. Mercredi's reaction once the accord had been rejected was indicative of that. Canada had a chance to right its past with the Aboriginal peoples and blew it.

It's hard to be progressive today, because it no longer means the same thing as it did in modern times. Sometimes, the more progressive we are, the more we get into a jam. Defending individual rights is progressive. No one I know would want to do without them. But it isn't enough, and sometimes it isn't even helpful, to solve other problems. Sometimes, too, being progressive on other issues puts you at loggerheads with individual rights. Recognizing the distinct nature of Québec and Aboriginal societies, for example. The Reform Party understands that, but resolves the problem by forgetting about certain differences: Québec's, among others, reducing the problem of French to a question of need and cost-effectiveness. Or in its attitude to immigration, where it would base immigration policy on Canada's economic needs, thereby wiping out any problem of racism, conveniently forgetting that the people who might most want to immigrate come from countries where the economies are poor and the régimes often repressive. One solves the question of discrimination on grounds of skin colour by changing the rules. Or states that the party welcomes genuine refugees, thereby implying that many refugees are not, enough certainly to warrant another change in the rules. Mr. Manning is not a systems analyst for nothing. Yet he is surprised that people consider his party right-wing. He too feels the world is no longer divided by the political categories of the French Revolution. Post-modernity, however, is an open house. One can make all kinds of combinations, including a systems analyst putting on populist robes. Including new forms of racism.

People think racism has to do with blacks and whites, hate on the basis of skin pigmentation. That's how it classically appeared in the early post-modern era — yes, postmodern, de Gobineau's treatise on the racial origins of inequality dates from the mid-nineteenth century — but as Colette Guillaumin pointed out, you can turn anything into racist categories; the trick is to give the outgroup a fixed character. Skin is good because it is genetic and so smacks of biology, letting people get into interminable and pointless debates over whether blacks are smarter or dumber than whites, as if that could explain something about who gets what. What they are arguing about is the nature of inequality and the way to justify it. Any explanation that enables people to say that things are as they are because people are like that, it's their different nature, fixes social convention in the bedrock of immutable categories. It's a way of thinking in racist terms about social arrangements. Even economic categories can become racist. Even categories like competence. In our society, for example, positions are allocated supposedly according to competence. Half of what happens to people is probably due to luck, and the rest is far from due to higher education diplomas. So competence serves a function of letting people think that if you are where you are, it's because you got it, the competence displayed by professionals at the top of the occupational ladder. As we go down the ladder, the hard-core competence gets harder to find. If we look for the competence of the people who came up with the Charlottetown deal, we'd also be hard pressed to find it.

We have to be careful. Post-modernity creates confusion as well as realignment. It is easy to tap into discontent and make everything seem self-evident, but as real as the discontent is, it's far from evident what to do about it. Much contemporary populism feeds off what the managers produce as a particular form of rationality, but their answers are not all that different. It is not self-evident to me that language in Canada is simply a question of getting service. It's not at all clear that language is about that anywhere. But in post-modern society, everything is usually seen as an instrument to something else. Life as a permanent tourist junket. Remember when they told us that we had to get the constitution settled in order to get on to other problems, like the economy? Not that they were entirely wrong. One reason for giving ourselves a constitution is to have a framework within which to deal with those other problems. But when the vote came in no and the government consoled itself by saying it would indeed now turn its attention to the economy, the first major piece of legislation turned out to be a cut in the unemployment insurance program. Millions of people out of work and Mr. Valcourt tells us we have to catch the abusers. Weed them out from the genuinely unemployed. When trade unions in Québec demonstrated in protest, he accused them of playing politics. I wonder what he thinks politics is about. Management, no doubt. Listening to that on the boob tube, you can really go crazy.

Post-modern society makes people crazy. The old categories don't apply but we still use them. At the level of behaviour we respond more and more to the pressures that come from a system that seems constantly to escape us. In doing so we enhance it, until something gives and we register, however we are able, that we think it's all so unreasonable. That's what Charlottetown was all about. No one was against all those good intentions, but the end result seemed to make no sense. Especially after months and years of working us up to a point where it did feel as if the country were coming apart, as if we could no longer rely on the basic institutional framework within which we led our lives. The road to Charlottetown was turning into a revolution in reverse, a coming apart at the seams. And the more you thought about it, the more questions there were, since everybody seemed both right and wrong, everybody seemed to speak in code, love thy neighbour but don't give an inch. As I looked around I remember thinking: what are we all doing here? What am I doing here? How will we ever put all these differences together in some kind of reasonable civilized manner? What is civilized about it anyway, since everybody uses arguments to justify practices that have little to do with their ethical stance? That's post-modernism, is it not, a society with no overarching ethic. God is dead and we are floundering in a permanent state of anxiety; and no valium. Realism means understanding everybody really hates each other. Educated, uneducated, we're all the same, Mr. Rousseau. And then came the accord, inept and well-meaning, such that yes and no diminished in importance. And I thought: Canada, that's life; and meant by that, life in general and post-modern life in particular. For we are the first post-modern state, the first society to try and found itself on the terrain of difference which makes social foundation so difficult. Nothing from the past will really work. We'll have to think it through in new ways. That's what a constitution means, after all.

PART

TWO

THOMAS HOBBES WAS BORN when Elizabeth I still reigned over England. He lived for most of the seventeenth century and elaborated certainly one of the most penetrating political philosophies of modernity. His most famous work is *Leviathan*. There he developed the idea that society rested on a social contract, but instead of justifying liberal democracy, Hobbes argued that the social contract underlay, and legitimated, absolutism. He argued that when people agreed to place themselves under a sovereign power, or in other words to live together in society, they did so on the understanding that the sovereign would protect them, guarantee them security of their person. For security of their person was the reason why people got together in the first place; otherwise they could live in a state of nature. But Hobbes knew that in the state of nature life was nasty, brutish and short.

The state of nature was a mythical construct. No one has ever seen human beings in that state, just as no one has ever been to paradise. But the social contract was no less real. People didn't get together and draw up an agreement to live together. They were born into society. What Hobbes was doing was to try and reflect on what held society together when it could no longer be assumed that it was divine will that ordered the nature of human relationships in organized fashion. That was typical of a modern mind, which seeks to reflect on what human beings ought to do in order to do what they have to do. In exploring the nature of the social contract, Hobbes was pointing out what even traditional society had known: human beings get together in order to live in civilized fashion. Otherwise, social life is a reign of terror, the strong against the weak, passion unbridled and flailing out in all directions, a cycle of murder and revenge. That was why Hobbes was willing to concede to the sovereign absolute power, for his power rested on his capacity to guarantee his subjects the security that life would be conducted according to principles of justice, which meant codes of conduct rather than whim.

Restraint, not caprice. Which made even the absolute sovereign subject to behaviour that was not purely arbitrary. It was a short step from there to giving subjects rights, formalizing them in ways that limited the sovereign power and assured each citizen due process of law. Indeed, Hobbes's argument underscores the extent to which the modern doctrine of rights was embedded in the modern state. It also shows that even under modernity, even with the emergence of the individual as a social and existential character, the parameters of the social question still revolve around society, not the individual. As they must, whatever we may think in post-modern times.

This was one of the reasons why Hobbes was so much more powerful a thinker than Rousseau. One reads him and knows right away he had no illusions about the human condition. He had read his Bible, as had Freud, that other great thinker who appeared on the stage of modernity, but this time as it drew to a close. They understood that society was founded on crime. This does not mean that society is organized murder. It does mean that society emerges in order to allow human beings to live in other than criminal ways. Lawless behaviour is behaviour outside society. That is why, in modern society, one didn't give the vote to criminals. They had no rights because they had placed themselves outside the social order by violating its contract. Only in post-modern times, when we no longer understand what society is about, do we give them the right to vote, just as we now give it to mental patients. It may sound progressive, but if that's progress, may God forgive us. The gesture is tantamount to saying there's no harm in society's being run by idiots. Isn't there? What about the old saying, you don't put the fox in charge of the chicken coop? But maybe post-modern society is a form of collective idiocy.

Why do I go back to Hobbes? Because he points me in the right direction. When I look at the world I live in and wonder how we will put all those differences together, he reminds me of what it is that we do when we form a society. We are creating the conditions that make people feel secure. Peace, order and good government, as our Constitution puts it. Machiavelli understood that even for his prince. Otherwise it's Cain and Abel, Sodom and Gomorrah. No sooner had God created the world and human beings set about their business than the first family produces crime. Cain, jealous, kills his brother and then cringes before God for his life, asks for a mark that will enable him to go among men and so arrest the spiral of retaliation before it starts. But human beings in those days had as much trouble getting off to a decent start as post-modern Canadians. Things go so badly even God decides to start over. A few chapters after the flood, Abraham is bargaining with God to spare Sodom if he can find ten just men in the city. Just men. For Sodom's crime was it had no justice. Visitors would come and be robbed, beaten, raped, violating the fundamental rules of hospitality: how to make the stranger welcome, recognize the bond despite the difference, turn the wild into the civil.

Of course every act of foundation has its arbitrary side. That's why every revolution is a form of parricide. Perhaps that's why in traditional society foundation was anchored in divine ordinance. God is by nature arbitrary. Humans, on the other hand, cannot afford that, are under obligation to set rules. That's why they are not gods, and why it is folly to try and become one. Folly as in madness, as the French would have it. Thou shalt not kill becomes the cornerstone of human society. To kill is to step over the limit, cross the boundary, as Pierre Legendre reminded us in his study of Corporal Lortie's crime. That's what makes it hard pleading insanity to murder. Murder by definition is insane. In his study, Legendre pointed out there are two ways of reproducing madness within that first unit of human community, the family. One is by the father himself stepping over the line and committing incest. The other is by absconding, turning the family into a purely functional unit, where rights and power relations are managed by a consortium of age groups, therapists, schools, social workers, television stations and shopping plazas. As if we could abolish the arbitrary and a human response to it: that adults become parents and don't step over the line; instead defend it by exercising authority. In the name of society. In the name, if need be, of God who made man and woman in His image.

So I look at Canada's constitutional mess, remember Hobbes, meditate on the Bible, and think that the purpose of any constitution is to elaborate a government that assures the citizens security to their person. It is not to promote the particular rights of diverse social categories. It is to make people feel at home, as much as one can feel at home in this cosmos; to let them know that they are protected from arbitrary vandalism wreaked on body or soul by neighbour or state; to assure them there is justice in the world and they can appeal to it. In this respect, the idea of individual rights represented a major conquest for humanity, and there are not many in our sojourn on this planet. It extended the covenant of traditional society into a social contract, limiting even the sovereign's power in new and forceful ways. The danger that threatens us today is that we want to do without the sovereign, reduce its power to an instrument to promote the emancipation of every social category. A dangerous enterprise, for it means that every social institution will be treated in like fashion. Our multiple differences become means to attack authority everywhere, but without authority, legitimately acknowledged power, there is no justice. People freak out, become insecure, turn violent, even if it's civilized violence, the kind that goes on inside the city, among its own inhabitants, within every institution.

So what do we do about the rest? What do we do about French and English? What do we do about Aboriginals and their discontent? What do we do about all the groups clamouring about discrimination and demanding positive action? We look backwards, try and think what justice means as we do today what Hobbes did for his time. There have not been a thousand formulations in the course of human history. One has been to think of justice in terms of God. Another has sought it in terms of reason and natural law. The second can be understood as an attempt to found human affairs on grounds that appear rational to the human mind as it thinks self-critically about our place in the universe. In that scientific, materialist approach, as the modern effort has come to be qualified, we have tried to think politically in terms of some first law, some absolute axiom like two and two make four; as if all subsequent developments would flow logically from that. But life is much more complicated, as we have known for a long time. Between the Bible and Freud stood Shakespeare, reminding us there are more things in heaven and earth than are dreamed of in our philosophies. Which is why a new step in self-critical thought has to think not only in terms of first principles, but also in terms of history. That is the positive side of post-modernism.

There are people who think we have nothing to learn from history. They think it is bunk, subjective, a demiurge Maoists invoke to justify great leaps forward. But it is also our past; and for the first time it is coming to be our universal heritage. In the Royal Ontario Museum you can move from Babylon to Art Deco simply by changing rooms, often only by shifting your gaze. People read the National Geographic while sitting on the pot. If they're starving in Somalia you're bound to know about it. You're even bound to know that the situation is worse in the Sudan. Every big city is a source of illumination on a scale Rimbaud might have found dizzying. Not only can we all travel as Goethe did. We can voyage in time in a way our predecessors could not. History has become a vast archaeological dig, so that we have a laboratory of human experience from which to draw conclusions and a measuring stick of no mean proportions in trying to decide what is important. In short, history, and our critical reflection upon it, might do for us what reason did for the modern philosophers. In the light of history we might learn what it is to be reasonable, and that is not always the same thing as being rational or right, at least not in the mathematical sense.

So I look back at history the way Tennyson's hero looked to the future and I too see it all, see the blood and the gore and the litany of broken promises, yet still the attempt to cradle life, to raise us all one step above the inanimate and recognize what can also be seen as a prison but is not, for it's only our condition: the need to make sense, render whole, seek order and lay it down, for that is our job on this spidery arm of a galaxy hanging in space and time as if history were the museum that it is. And as I already wrote, there are not fifty ways, only every epoch, if it is lucky, trying to go pass the mark, give itself rules that make it live beyond what it ever can do. Do justice, love mercy, walk humbly with thy God. Or Hadrian, trying to restore order to an empire we and he know will crumble. Just like ours, just like this entire society that cannot go on forever, because nothing does, and all the more so when it gives up on trying to make sense in the first place. And I ask myself what makes sense, and for that too I look to the past, since no one is going to invent the wheel, only show us in new language what humans have always known: how we love and lust, let the blood come thundering to the heart and raise the hand in betrayal, and when it is over allow the tongue to speak, the ancient poet celebrating the sack of Troy and today's retelling the story, and however much the roles change and everyone brought equal to everyone else, the same heart will invent a way to play out the drama on new terrain, and once again we will need to throw up the ramparts, put a fence around our lives, and the fence like a mirror so we can see what we are doing.

We think we are locked onto progress, but what progress there is crawls like a snail and measures itself with the pace of centuries. Millenniums. Two thousand years to abolish slavery, even after we know it is wrong. And yet it's done, and now become part of human consciousness right around the globe. Some small measure of satisfaction, some tiny indication that as history moves it moves into universality, brings us all within the commonality of our experience. That too is what it means to live in a global village; people in faraway countries writing letters to tyrants, asking for amnesty for political prisoners and sometimes even succeeding, because the tyrants also send representatives to the parliament of the world. Not much, it is true, hardly a dent in the sum of human misery, but better than six cities of refuge in a strip of land on the Mediterranean. And this great and long and hopeless scale of moral progress there to give us an idea, to measure up what is worth defending and what to let slide by the boards, for when it comes down to the essentials, what more is there to do than to do what we can with the means at our disposal so that care throws its mantle over the world?

And so, when we think of a constitution, what more can we seek to lay out as first principles than what we have painfully learned is needed? Peace in the land, security in the person, solidarity among society's members. They are needed because without them nothing can be done, nothing transmitted, that really holds anything of value. A museum is not a warehouse of destruction, and though we count the dead, we do so with regret, not celebration. It is enough that death is at life's perimeter, a reminder of that which we struggle against, the pain of wanton violence. And we do so because we give birth, because children enter the world and to them we tell stories that transform the pain, and when we are adult, build temples that transform ours. That's why people visit the Parthenon and even James Bay.

I drove up to James Bay once, right up through the largest municipality in the world. There is one stop be-

tween the entrance to the town and the hydro-electric station 600 kilometres north. The stop too is known by its
measure: kilometre 381. The further north you go the
more the earth joins the sky. The landscape becomes taiga,
short shrub on flat bare rock, that melts into the horizon
like water. You look at the sky and see puddles, after a
while can no longer make out what is cloud and what
belongs to the depths. The land becomes purple, and as the
sun sets, the sky turns into an idea of endless I have seen
nowhere else. By the time the power station came into
view night had foreclosed on the world. Above countless
stars and in front an eerie lit up landscape, orange electric,
strangely beautiful in this dry blackness, like a kid's huge
mecano set, and oddly voluptuous. In the daylight you get
to see the dam at LG-2. The construction is awesome, immense stairs over which the overflow would rush should
the water level rise too high. The stairs are hewn out of
mountain and river, climb upward the way you imagine
them at a temple of antiquity, a highway to heaven they
don't show on television. The bus that gives you the
guided tour drives right along the lake, over a constructed
causeway that leads into the power station itself, carved
into the rock that holds the dam. One is in the bowels of
the beast. Sixteen immense turbines all lined up in a room
the size of a stadium, each with hundreds of magnets
placed just right or the turbines do not move. The scale is
colossal, and it all came out of a human mind. I am impressed. With all the talk and controversy I was not expect-
ing this. Whatever else has been done, it is beautiful. A
monument we have created, like the Agora in Athens, or
the pyramids in Egypt, or what is left from the Aztecs. It
would take half of New York to rival it. Like all the other
monuments, it was achieved at great cost. People paid,
maybe even a way of life.

To get to James Bay itself you have to drive another hour.
West of LG-2. The country is softer, gives off the feel of a
human touch. A little past Fort Chissassibi you finally

come to water and disappointment. The bay is completely indented, so you see not a great expanse but a little pond and row-boats upturned on land. There is something beautiful about this too, this landscape that could have been painted by Seurat and where people come for work, love, evening prayer, as people have been coming to places like this for thousands of years. I know this has little to do with running the gauntlet of nature and the loud disputes that have echoed across the entire province all the way to Ottawa, but these two images are stuck in my mind when I think of what the country looks like and how much beauty is hiding in all that desolate geography. And I think of Glenn Gould who caught something of that in northern Ontario as he drove on highway 17 listening to Petula Clark sing *Who Am I?* on the radio. Marathon, Terrace Bay, they too were excuses to meditate, on what music and suburbia could do to the human mind. And driving down from James Bay you could listen to Gould over and over, trying to fathom what he had distilled from J.S. Bach, dead now for over two centuries. And you think: Glenn Gould playing the Goldberg Variations is reason enough for this country having existed.

So maybe now, when every detour leads to another canvas, such that all our actions seem incomplete until, in the reflective light, someone says it is good meaning beautiful, maybe now the time has come to put beauty in the constitution. Perhaps that will be post-modernity's contribution to the way we think about human government, discovering beneath all that ranting about autonomy a principle that hitherto was considered ethics' country cousin. For isn't that what lies behind contemporary society's tremendous appeal, behind the countless fabrics and the halogen lamps and the cordless telephones and everything else we think of as the artefacts of progress, even up to the triple bypasses and organ transplants, all of that really there so we can say we have lived to see this and this and this, one more angle of light on the human predicament that will open our eyes before we shut them for good? Isn't it only under today's conditions that we can begin to think consciously about life as essentially an aesthetic experience and not simply a hamper of goods, not even a hamper of rights, because the hamper is actually quite full?

Imagine a Canada Clause that read: Canadians and their governments are committed to a beautiful society, consider that social policy should conform to the principles of harmony, elegance, sublime beauty. Just like LG-2. Just like the Parthenon. Just like the mathematical equation for relativity or Bach's Goldberg Variations. For they all have harmony, some basic element of just proportion which must be there in every work of art or it somehow fails. A society is really not any different. It too requires balance, proportion, as does the justice it must mete out. Which makes government an art, not a science, and certainly not a program of operational procedures. Perhaps if, in mapping out their actions, our leaders used beauty, and not simply pragmatic efficiency, the Charlottetown accord might have looked different. And so too would the nightly news. Perhaps we would be spared an ever-growing complexity that simply looks like a mess. Perhaps we would not hear, now that child abuse and sexual harassment have made it on and off the agenda, that elder abuse is next, a growing Canadian problem which must be addressed, for which the government is willing to do its part: send educational material with the old-age pensions so that kids who are robbing their elders blind can read that it's a no-no. If you believed the media, the contemporary family is the most dangerous place in the world. Perhaps their problem is they've never read the Bible. Or maybe Jacob's problem was a lack of social workers.

Beauty. Simplicity. Like universal social services. Something everyone can understand and is willing to defend. They make sense, they are reasonable, they refer us all to our common humanity. They are also the tried and true product of history, which also makes them reasonable by virtue of experience. Ask anyone old enough to remember what it was like without medicare. Ask anyone to imagine what it could be like. And yet we move in that direction as we opt for more and more costly procedures, whose net effect is more likely to dent the social contract than measurably improve the quality of our lives. But in the absence of some socially generated standards, we let the techniques define the purpose. It's easier, it's pragmatic, it's a matter of numbers; but in the process we are moving to a society stratified along every conceivable line: money, age, job, skin colour, fullness of limbs, country of origin, food you eat, temple you pray in, music you listen to, holidays, retirement package, sexual partner, marital status, type of illness, alas even type of terminal illness. And so the society becomes more complex in exactly the wrong way, the kind that produces an aesthetic nightmare. Which makes for bad politics. Reasonable is made to appear simple-minded while we lurch from crisis to crisis. It has become a way of life to which everyone adapts, not least the technocrats whose job is to organize it. Perhaps that's why they are indispensable; they manage our insecurity on a permanent basis.

Still, I think we should be reasonable. It's easier than trying to manage, and making the country a work of art is an idea I highly approve. In the case of Canada even the questions are fairly simple. We know what really bugs us, what sticks in the throat beyond the carping of Calgary's oilmen and the ambition of the directors of the *Caisses Desjardins*. We have some things to clear up from the past. We have to make English-speaking and French-speaking Canadians feel at home, secure, not constantly suspicious that the other major linguistic group is there to gnaw away at that elusive identity which used to be assumed, but now has to be defended to be found. And since the French have somewhat less to fall back on in this free trade area called North America, it is perhaps worth going on record that

Canada is in favour of both. Canadians and their governments. Now that the railroads are going broke, perhaps we
can use language to bind us coast to coast, see to it that
three generations down the line everyone can speak at least
these two tongues. Speak them well too, not simply in
order to get by when stuck in political traffic. Which
means we have to educate our offspring, teach them what
culture is all about: Racine and Eliot and Proust and Joyce
and even some of our home-made contributors to what is
called civilization. And if they know that, they might also
know the principles of modern science and why Barnett
Newman in the National Gallery is something to be proud
of. We might stop complaining that we are not producing
enough brain power to compete in this increasingly competitive world. We might even retain the brains we
produce, since they might appreciate living in a society
whose leaders reflect polish and class and a goodly measure
of understanding, themselves having learned the meaning
of difference in their own glottal stops.

It's an elegant solution however you look at it. We make
amends for all those wrongs of the past, those that are real
and those imagined. We also recognize our own history, the
one going back to Cartier and Champlain, to Cabot and
Lasalle, to La Vérendrye and Fraser, and that has worked
its way down the centuries of marriage and conflict so that
we are stuck, happily and mercifully stuck with it. That is
important: to recognize rather than to master cognitively.
The latter is knowledge, but the former is the understanding that surpasseth knowledge; just what is implied
by historical consciousness as a step away, a step back-
ward, from the mania of getting everything under control
and in the end controlling so little, not even a country
from falling apart. Of course we would have less to
grumble about. We would have to give up the chewed-over
ball of yarn that has by now become so familiar; but sometimes in the course of human history it is good to change

the object of one's worry and find another dispute to ease oneself into boredom.

Then, too, consider this: we would be telling the people who for so long have been saying it makes no economic or any other sense for people in Nanaimo or Come-By-Chance to speak the king's French, that we think it does, because we have another idea of sense, what makes a life good, a person intelligent, a past worth preserving, a past long and broad enough to turn it into a society. What holds for Timmins holds for Chicoutimi, and who knows where the Mavis Gallant of 2070 will come from?

And if we could do that much for ourselves, perhaps we could also do it for the Aboriginals, the Inuits and the Indians who stalked and inhabited and worshipped this land long before Europeans came and in ways so different that it is hard for the post-modern mind really to get a handle on it. But this much we know, if only that too in the retrospect of history: that wrongs were committed we ought to stop and redress if they are to become part of the fabric, and not at the cost of their giving up what they are not ready to abandon. That also is a nice idea with its particular form of beauty, working out a way for two social mind-sets to inhabit the same space, taking the time to see how much electricity and natural gas we couldn't do without, balanced off against the caribou they hunt and paint and how poor we'd be if they didn't. It's a little hard to imagine except by watching Mr. Mercredi speak, slowly, calmly, all the time in the world underneath him like a carpet, no need to drop his voice into his diaphragm like stale carrot cake; every minute, like each little knot in constitutional negotiations, a reason unto itself.

If we did that, actually did it, made it so the three major historical communities involved in the emergence of Canada felt this land was theirs, because each knew it was also the work of the other's and together had worked out a political formula which recognized it, I bet everyone would feel a little more secure, would be less ready to use their rights to ensure they weren't being had. We'd be less worried that every arrangement that gave power to some took power away from the other, less quick to scrutinize our attempts to found a society from the viewpoint of how our rights were threatened. Without the foundation, and without the intent to establish it other than by adding and subtracting the desires of interest groups to a power of unknown proportions, we can only look forward to more insecurity. Hobbes was right and still is. Why else did some Canadians look at Charlottetown and all that preceded it and shake their heads in amazement, thinking of Yugoslavia and what had become of it?

Let's not exaggerate, I could hear some people say. We are not like that, the hatreds don't run so deep, the scars haven't been hammered into memory by nearly half a century of ruthless centralism. And yet Yugoslavia became a metaphor, an example to be feared, a symbol of what happens when insecurity gets outside the psyche and lays its hands on power, guns, territory where lines are drawn over grievance. Division, subdivision, wrong piled upon wrong until one no longer need remember what precipitated the decline. Suddenly you are in a terrible mess and the mess feeds on itself, food for the hungry piling up at the airport outside the city and no one able to understand why, though people explain on the radio the political logic of it all.

I tend to agree with the people who say we should not exaggerate. I look around at the young people in this country and find enmity between English and French, between white and red and black, to be conspicuous, on the whole, by its absence, none of that subtle and not so subtle prejudice I can remember being part of the atmosphere my generation breathed in at a similar point in our lives. That does not mean things can't take a turn for the worse. It's just that the long-term trend points to danger from another direction. In the face of individual tolerance for diversity where difference is the spice of life, commonality becomes hard to fathom. That the absence of a defined political community can create insecurity of its own kind is a little harder to imagine in a world where insecurity is understood mainly as lacking an escape route. But if the legacy of tolerance which my generation has contributed to the saga of cellular development, wilfully, blindly, in spite of and because of LSD and feminism, is to set the world partially to right, then the society will also have to find a way to inscribe it politically in the charter that holds its members together. Read, or reread, *Leviathan* if you don't believe me. The old books are sometimes still the best.

Have you ever stopped to think what a country is? I mean really stopped, and really a country. I remember when we were kids, there was this story in our grade school reader about city mouse and country mouse, and then when I had kids, there was this other story about the little house in the country to which came the city, building around but not destroying it until its post-modern owners dragged it back to whence it came, the moral some kind of Marxist lesson about the separation between town and country. It blew my mind to see in some Toronto shopping centre that phrase town and country; it turned out to be a clothing chain store that recently went bankrupt. I was surprised to see it in Toronto. In some file of my Montréal childhood the name belonged to a dry cleaners in the shopping centre near our house; and although my brother had moved to Toronto, I didn't think he had taken the shopping centre with him. But you never know. A lot of the country goes down the 401. It's one of the complaints the Maritimes have, especially that the traffic is lopsidedly one-way.

Being from Québec, I get to travel the 401. My daughter goes to university in Kingston. Family and friends live in Toronto. Late in my life I went to visit Niagara Falls, when I realized that people from across the ocean made it, along with the Gaspé, a must on their Canadian trip. They were right; all that death-defying water and yellow raincoats to boot. But I like the 401 best. It is flat and low and the sky is always grey, even when the sun in summer wears down the eyes, and even in springtime it seems like autumn when you hardly have to look to see the birds fly south, black cadets in some semblance of formation, weaving down the river itself weaving before it spoons out into Lake Ontario and a thousand islands hiding from sight the wealth and glory of Upper Canada. At Rimouski the St. Lawrence gives a similar impression, suddenly becoming a broad expanse that turns a river into the sea; and there too you are suddenly surprised that this is part of your country, within its frontiers, you have but to drive and drive to see it all. And even then. And even what you see you are not sure is what you have seen, for the country is immense, a tableland of shield and lake that stretches right up to the North Pole, and for all its exhausting repetition there is invariably a moment of surprise, a length of road that leads into steeple, clapboard, village main street and then beyond where the soft air paws the sun, and even the grey turns to purple in the day moving to that hour between wolf and dog. If you ride the 401 late at night you can see the smoke climb into the sky as men and women take the night shift and turn the landscape into an industrial hallelujah. That too is strange, the way sweat and brow can pump into the air enough labour so that the vision beyond your windshield gets you thinking. "Heart-mysteries there", much like a country.

Not everyone would agree. Some think the country is an economy, as if somehow the economy were more real than a landscape that might very well be a picture. By economy they mean a market, a flow of goods and services their job is to control. Which they think they do. Ever since the Crash they think they do. Keynes, they say, the man who laid out the general theory that governors and their advisers think they use. We've all come to learn its basic assumptions: when times are good, the government builds up a surplus to soak up excess demand in the economy, and when times are bad, it builds up a deficit, spending to get the economy moving again. Only it doesn't work like that in practice, as the current situation shows only too well. And Keynes's theory was the most intelligent of the lot. To paraphrase what a wise man once told me, it's trickle-up economics that our society needs, for when millions buy, the wheels are bound to turn. Yet the wheels aren't turning, and most of the management seems like forecasting that is wider off the mark than the weather.

One reason that Keynesianism doesn't work is that in good times the government doesn't pile up the surpluses. It spends then too, since people demand, needs grow, and the politicians have to get re-elected. Our society also works that way. What's the point of progress if all that wealth can't lead us to afford a little more? Besides, if demands didn't trickle up from the bottom, problems would trickle down from the top. Creative solutions, these problems are called, forestalling what might be down the road. No one really controls the money supply, much the way no one controls anything else in a society that has lost a notion of boundaries. In the end, the economy becomes a myth, some disembodied drawing on graph paper that turns into a form of terrorism. No one really understands how it works, but it serves as a reason for a lot of things people are at a loss to explain. Why productive is never productive enough. Why the government can't manage growth or jobs. Why the insurance we paid out over the years cannot come back to us when we need it. Why, with more and more education and all the money spent on it, we don't get to see the payoff. Even the length of sentences shrinks, not to mention our competitive edge. Perhaps that's what happens when the economy bears less and less relation to the real amount of goods produced and real labour required to produce it. We live in a society where everybody has jobs but few people work; instead they manage, big and small, in one way or another, helping to deal with the difficulties of post-modern life. Maybe that's what is meant by defining the economy as aggregate demand. What I like best are the moments they explain that the problem is one of confidence. It's almost as if the cat's let out the bag: an economy is really a state of mind. Perhaps in post-modern times it is. Perhaps it always was.

Keynes, I suspect, knew that the economy was not even an economy. When he first proposed his unorthodox theories, that government should spend when times were rough, he defended his ideas against his critics, who argued he didn't take a long enough view, by reminding everyone that in the long run we are all dead. The remark is rather famous and owes its celebrity to the existential core it touches. What are we but beings of time, and time, at that, that is running out? A mystery there, the hardest of the lot; we to whom notice is given in advance nonetheless dream of eternity and invent mathematics with imaginary numbers. Perhaps Keynes wanted to tell us that an economy does not exist in a vacuum, cannot become the purpose of its own functioning, but production and consumption inscribe themselves within the contours of human life. Economy is nothing without a society and society is the social form within which human beings live, let time slip through their fingers, while it away and watch it while. But Keynes was a thinker, which just goes to show you can't run an economy without a philosophy.

So what about a country? Is it too a state of mind, and especially ours, some imaginary Zion past Dryden, Ontario, where the forest is so thick and black softness slips from the soul and you wonder how anything but terror can inhabit this land which was once invaded by glaciers? Or perhaps it is that canvas Constable might have painted you saw one afternoon in northern Manitoba, where the light fell quietly on fenced-in land and the cows lowed by small ponds and you stood by a bridge overlooking a creek and stared at this dun and green as if it were a gauze strip of forever. Then you drove on and hit Winnipeg, where you've been before so it's no surprise, but when you get back home and listen to the radio when As It Happens or The World At Six goes to Portage and Main for an interview, you do not think of the city you've been to but the one you've always had in your mind from the days Winnipeg was only a name, first attached to a football team and then, later, to a general strike. It's like *la conquête* in which you can hardly believe once you've actually been to the Plains of Abraham. The cliffs are so steep you cannot imagine how the British ever managed to take the city, until your friend explains that Montcalm was betrayed, and it suddenly clicks that this whole adventure we call Canada might simply be a history of betrayal. And you tell your friend how you were once in St. Louis and thought of Lasalle opening up the Mississippi and tried to imagine what it would have been like had French Canada held onto the Ohio Valley. The whole continent would have turned out differently as French pushed its way to the Pacific, but the successors to Colbert's France didn't understand what these *arpents* of snow were all about. Even before Montcalm was betrayed the dream of *Nouvelle France* had been abandoned. Only the memory remains to turn itself into a country.

Perhaps that's all Canada is and perhaps it is not even that, for this country is a host of memories, each one cased away in its dreams, each one murmuring to the night lines of consciousness its memory is not the one of its neighbours. When you sit down to think about it, the curtains drawn, the amber Scotch poured into the glass, this country, any country, hardly makes sense except as a dream. James Joyce once called Ireland an old sow that eats its farrow, a line worth more than all the nationalism in the world, will stay and stay long after the killing has stopped; and you think that if you press Canada to the wall of your own consciousness it too will disappear, turned by time into dust motes, footnotes, lines you have read in someone's poems, music on the compact disc that makes you think of Leipzig, Bach, a man trying to get all that sound on paper for the glory of God and the alimentary needs of his seventeen children. The more you think the more the world's solidity melts, leading you on, with every lick of drink and each turn in the variations, into that zone where what is and what is not stare at each other with all the force of the question mark you know is the very heart of the matter, and you wonder what the fuss is all about and think it a miracle and rather kind that so many people have gone out of their way to get so upset about nothing.

At that point you realize that Canada is the answer to its own question, is as much as anything else, which in the end is its great trump card. We all need a form and Canada is ours, having, in the course of its relatively young existence, drawn boundaries around a land, produced maps, stamps, provincial coats of arms, cities in Québec with names like Sherbrooke and streets called King, Queen, Québec, Ontario, Wellington, Kitchener, even High, not to mention the proverbial Montcalm and Wolfe and the Montréal it would like to be. Not so bad, you realize, better to fight your battles over street signs and accept that your country measures up fairly well against the bloodied drama of others; for it can always be worse, as any reasonable person knows when looking at a question mark.

Of course, it could also be better, and one gets to regret now and then that we are not more bold, less content with our national squabblings and a little more eager to try and make something of this not so bad inheritance. We could, too, if we used our strengths, decided indeed that they were strengths; like a country that did not lean too much on its inhabitants, was happy to be, just to be, and aimed now and then at adult viewing. Imagine Canada: the first post-modern state willing to do something about post-modernity. Imagine Canada: a country willing in part to be the imaginary country it actually is. Wreck Beach and north of Edmonton and an open air window looking to sea at some campground in Prince Edward Island. Or the Matapédia

Valley with ghost towns that refuse to die and rails running alongside a river where fishermen wade up to their thighs in order to keep summer real. And in water-logged northern Ontario, nearly smack in the middle of Lake Nipigon an island that carries the name of Shakespeare.

When I am sick I watch tv. When I come home late at night from work I also flick it on, hoping against hope that the Star Trek reruns have improved. I notice there are now late night ads for telephone sex on the same stations which earlier in the day pride themselves on family viewing. I know that in post-modern life we are able to harbour considerable role dissonance, a fancy term to mean, among other things, your job doesn't depend on whom you have sex with, but this midnight switch is a little much, kind of like affirmative action for the sexually challenged. It makes *Anne of Green Gables* look really good, which it is, but it could do without the comparison. Much of tv is air pollution and a terrible waste of natural resources, among which I include the human mind. It's too bad. I keep thinking of David Bowie in *The Man Who Fell To Earth*, that part when he said that television tells you the truth but not the whole truth. I keep watching for the whole truth, but I only get confused.

I much prefer the radio. You get so much more information for your listening money. You can also cook and eat your meals, which it's harder to do while watching television. You can also talk to the radio in your head, which you can't do with tv. It takes over and your only recourse is to shut it off. A friend of mine put his in his apartment locker. Solitary confinement. Another nice thing about radio is you really feel hooked up to the country, can understand what it must have meant in the thirties if you lived in some rural outpost and only the wireless to keep you in touch. In the long historical perspective, radio really brought about the transformation. Conceptually, most tv is still radio plus pictures. Perhaps if they only showed the pictures.

If I'm home at noon and it all works out, I listen to the hot line show as I eat. Tuning in on the world, I call it, just to make sure I keep abreast, check it still works the way I think it does. Today, for example, where the subject of discussion was how to protect your kids from abduction. On the tv last night, there was a documentary about some two-year-old in Liverpool who wandered away from his mother in a shopping centre and wound up dead. A horrible story from all its angles, all caught on a video camera, but as the show's announcer said, the purpose of using it for today's discussion was not to rake us over our angst, it was to see how people protect their children without putting them in a strait-jacket. The calls then proceeded to pour in and we were all raked over our angst. To listen to the stories people had to tell, you'd be scared to take your kids shopping. One woman called in to say precisely that: before she gets out of the car she goes over the rules with all her kids. The father of a child who had disappeared lamented the fact that nowadays, children will not grow up with the easy childhood that had been his. A mother phoned in to say that in her community there is a school program, starting in kindergarten, to make children feel good about themselves and their bodies, and to empower them not to do anything they don't feel comfortable doing. Another woman reported that, living in the country, she doesn't let her child play out of her sight down the lane on their own property. As the man said, childhood is no longer the same. But then, neither is our world.

I listened to all this while trying to eat and heard the way we speak work its poison. So you're guilty if your kid gets murdered by maniacs and you're guilty if your kid is over-protected and you're guilty if your kid is under-empowered and this isn't meant to be a trip, but all that people share is their worry and confusion and everyone admitting, yes it is a problem, and I think: just like child abuse, flooded over the airwaves a while ago; it's not safe in the home, it's not safe in the streets, and it's no longer safe in the confines of your mind. On top of which there's always someone to tell you it's always been like this, the only difference now is it's talked about. Pretty soon there will be a new quiz show: who's coming out of the closet tonight? Something is wrong, definitely wrong, but it's not what it seems, not even what I recount. I think it's the idea that this is a problem, that we think this is a problem that can somehow be dealt with, managed, we can share some techniques, when all that we share is our terrible sympathy for the parents who have had to go through this ordeal and relief for those who can tell of close calls. Yet we pay for this little shot of emotion with the words that go in with the best intentions. Words, words, words, said Hamlet, but soon we will all be mad north by northwest.

There is something novel about a society that lives through its media. Everything happens through the interface of clumps of reality that are always a relay to something else. If, in the end, life becomes art, it's because life now tries to imitate the representation we have imagined; but what we imagine has little to do with the wellsprings of the soul, with the flow of time over the flesh that registers the ineffable and seeks for it, waits for it, hopes as we imagine the stars hope, knowing they are balls of fire and gas but not letting that interfere, for when we look at them they do twinkle; why else would Mozart have composed? No, what we imagine is how to master the reality to which we have shrunk life, agendas within agendas, each complete with its strategy; and the sharp people know it, on and off the television that consecrates them. Maybe that's what the man who fell to earth was trying to say: there's a whole society out there, for which these screens of high definition are a stand-in, a way of life like call waiting, for people who don't know how to wait. But then again, why wait? Haven't people been saying for years: why wait for spring, do it now?

That's what makes post-modernity so odd. It seems like the final stage-post of history, the culmination of all those proverbs which can finally mean something, since now so much of their advice is technically feasible. Yet it is also seen as the proverb's last hurrah, that moment when we can all kick over the traipses and bid those silly sayings of authority good-bye. In the name of emancipation. Empowerment. Self-actualization. Or that favourite expression, taking control. Even when we've lost control of the streets, as one man on that noon radio program cried through his cellular telephone. But maybe that's only a post-modern proverb to be taken with at least a grain of salt. Perhaps the trick is as it always was, to think the epoch against itself as much as you are for it. Maybe that's how you see the whole truth, which is not a truth but a paradox.

Like life. You know, what you think of in the still hours of the night, jazz on the radio or those old songs where time goes by, maybe Sarah Vaughan singing some ballad of pain that sounds terrific, and your mind trips out on all those scenes you never get to play in, *l'hiver de force* in either language, but then you remember that if you look at things right, it's always been *l'hiver de force*, and nothing really stops you. Of course, it's not exactly as it is in the book; a person's missing, or the late night films, or the bag of chips, but there are so many ways to arrive at laughter, stare in the face the absurdity of it all yet still love it, down to the inchworm kids sing about, it being all God's little creatures, even your fury and spite that the world is not unfolding as it should though doubtless the universe is.

Just like Canada. That's why I like it. If nothing else, it's a reminder about the incomprehensible knot at the centre of things. In many respects it is hard to figure out. You know it's there, but it rarely asserts itself in a conspicuous way. It's like those restaurant signs for Canadian dishes; you wonder what it means aside from a bacon, lettuce and tomato sandwich. But you know that outside the country people look on it kindly, almost enviously: peace, order and good government, a vast continent where they'll find their shack and possibly a refuge from misery and murder, working federalism with some problems. On the inside you move back and forth, liking the rather low profile, the golds and auburns in September and the blue February skies, and yet resenting its nearly shameful diffidence, the way its heroes always come lately and on their own, as if the country were indeed run by remittance men. Well, you think, it's post-modern before its time, and like the British Empire, in absence of mind; perhaps that's why it's constantly coming apart. And that too has its nice touch, a country never sure of itself and so always asking what is a country, which in the end is hardly more than a collection of graves, grass over bones to help the living.

So it is a mystery; at least defending it is. And yet I notice I have come to like it, this immense piece of permafrost that no one really gets excited over except when they want to divide it up. I should even be sorry to see that happen. I'd have to start thinking about my new country the way everybody else thinks of theirs, as people have been thinking about them now for centuries, strong nation-states with firm muscle tone, wedded to compact identity that is everywhere turning into picture books for coffee tables. And I think: better to take up the challenge of doing something with what you have, since anything else is only going to be a duplication of what already is. English Canada, Québec, even the Mohawk nation cannot resist the tides of history. They too will be forced to deal with difference clamouring for emancipation, drug abuse, teen-age suicide, corporate business planning for the future, incest crawling onto tv for mid-afternoon show and tell, and late at night a shocking revelation about long gone incidents to justify the present. Besides, Canada is already ahead of the game, having posed the problem in its most benign form and living with it for decades now, though others would say for centuries.

But not only that. By flattening itself into a country that refuses to be one, it has also posed the paradox of our need for a country even as we would do without one. John Lennon's *Imagine*; and all our lives heading into the future. And since a paradox really requires no answer, when people ask me why I'm in favour of Canada, I tell them because we have the Rockies and I'd like to keep it that way.

Selected Bibliography

Hannah Arendt, *On Revolution*, Viking, 1965.

John Berger, "The Moment of Cubism" in *The Look of Things*, Viking, 1974.

Elias Canetti, *Crowds and Power*, Farrar, Straus, Giroux, 1984.

Réjean Ducharme, *Dévadé*, Gallimard/Lacombe, 1990.

Réjean Ducharme, *L'hiver de force*, Gallimard, 1973.

Eugène Enriquez, *De la horde à l'Etat*, Gallimard, 1983.

Michel Freitag, *Dialectique et société, vol. 2, Les modes de reproduction formels de la société*, Editions Saint-Martin, 1986.

Michel Freitag, *"Discours idéologiques et langage totalitaire: quelques considérations actuelles sur le fascisme et son idéologie"*, in *Revue européenne des sciences sociales*, 21, 1983.

Mavis Gallant, *Home Truths: Selected Canadian Stories*, Macmillan, 1981.

Glenn Gould, "The Search for Petula Clark" in *From Ink Lake, Canadian Stories Selected by Michael Ondaatje*, Viking Penguin, 1990.

Colette Guillaumin, *L'idéologie raciste*, Mouton, 1972.

Raul Hilberg, *The Destruction of the European Jews*, Holmes and Meier, 1985.

Holling Clancy Holling, *Paddle-to-the-Sea*, Houghton Mifflin, 1941.

Thomas Hobbes, *Leviathan*.

Homer, *The Iliad*, (Richard Lattimore translation), University of Chicago Press, 1961.

James Joyce, *A Portrait of the Artist as a Young Man*, Penguin, 1977.

Margaret Laurence, *The Diviners*, McClelland and Stewart, 1974.

Pierre Legendre, *Le crime du caporal Lortie*, Fayard, 1989.

Robert Jay Lifton, *The Nazi Doctors*, Basic, 1986.

Christopher Logue, *War Music*, Farrar, Straus, Giroux, 1987.

Christopher Logue, *Kings*, Farrar, Straus, Giroux, 1991.

Karl Marx and Friedrich Engels, *The Communist Manifesto*.

The Old Testament.

Michael Ondaatje, *In the Skin of a Lion*, McClelland and Stewart, 1987.

Rainer Maria Rilke, *The Notebooks of Malte Laurids Brigge*, Viking, 1985.

William Shakespeare, *Hamlet*.

Société, a journal of critical theory on post-modernity, nos. 1-11, Département de sociologie, Université du Québec à Montréal, Groupe autonome d'édition, Montréal.

Alfred, Lord Tennyson, *Locksley Hall and Other Poems*, Kegan Paul, 1883.

Max Weber, *The Protestant Ethic and the Spirit of Capitalism*, Unwin, 1965.

William Butler Yeats, "The Second Coming" and "The Circus Animals' Desertion" in *Selected Poems*, edited by M. L. Rosenthal, Collier, 1966.

A. B. Yehoshua, *A Late Divorce*, Doubleday, 1984.

Marguerite Yourcenar, *Mémoires d'Hadrien*, Gallimard, 1974.